*His Highness Sheikh Hamad Bin Khalifa Al Thani*
*Emir of Qatar*

*His Highness Sheikh Tamim Bin Hamad Al Thani*
*Heir Apparent*

# QATAR

# QATAR

STACEY INTERNATIONAL

**Stacey International**
128 Kensington Church Street
London W8 4BH
Tel: +44-20 7221 7166, fax: +44-20 7792 9288
Email: enquiries@stacey-internationa.co.uk
www.stacey-international.co.uk

© Stacey International 2006

First published 2000
Revised edition 2006

**ISBN 1905299-05-2**

**Editor, this edition: David Chaddock**

Author team: Stephen Day CMG, Gina Coleman, Fran Gillespie, Michael Barron, with special thanks
for support and editorial guidance to Hussain Ahmed Al-Homaid and Abdul Moneim Hussein.

Designed by Kitty Carruthers
Printed and bound in China by SNP Leefung

**British Library Cataloguing in Publication Data.** A catalogue record for this title is available from the
British Library.

Picture credits:

All Stacey International except: Al Jazeera 92c&br; Associated Press 78, 79; Lars Bjorstrom 14ml,
15c(2), 16(2); Prof W Buttiker 14t; David Gillespie 9b, 10, 15 t,bl&r, 39(4), 66-7, 73r; Department of
Antiquities 38(2), 40(2), 41, 46t, 48-49; Doha Asian Games Organising Committee 140t &bl, 141tl;
Doha English Speaking School 120; Doha Ethnographic Museum 67t; Doha Golf Club 135t; Doha
Palace Archives 62-3; ERDWA 13bl; Hanne & Jenne Eriksen 13r3; Four Seasons Hotel 117l; John
Herbert 4 (br), 18, 19, 20b(2), 29(3), 28-9(6), 34b, 54-55, 83r, 90-1, 94t, 104-5, 114b; H Jungius
14bl; J Marsham 14bc; The Pearl 26(2); P Phelan 14br; Popperphoto 117, 138-9, 140m, 141r(3);
QAFCO, 108-9; QAPCO 84-5, 96-97, 98, 100-101, 106-7; Qatar Airways 88(4); Qatar Foundation
126, 127(2), 147; Qatar Gas 99; Qatar Ministry of Foreign Affairs: title page, vi, 1, 5, 20t, 24(2), 25t,
27, 30t, 37b, 43t, 45b, 50-51, 74, 75, 76, 80-81, 89(2), 95, 114t, 115, 121(3),122b, 123, 133t&b,
140-1b, 144-5(3); Qatar National Museum 23(5); Qatar Tourism Authority 8-9, 10-11, 25b, 32t, 36b,
66t, 67(2), 177b, 131, 132t&b, 135b, 134 t&b, 136(2), 137; Ritz Carlton Hotel 116r; Rydges Hotel
116tl, Dr Muhammad Tayat 12b.

*Half title page:* At a nationally rally, a young Qatari clutches a furled flag.
*Title page:* The clock tower seen here at eventide beside the Central Mosque is one of the oldest
          monuments in Doha.
*Opposite:* Qatar's seafaring heritage is kept alive today: a boum skipper tends his craft.

# Contents

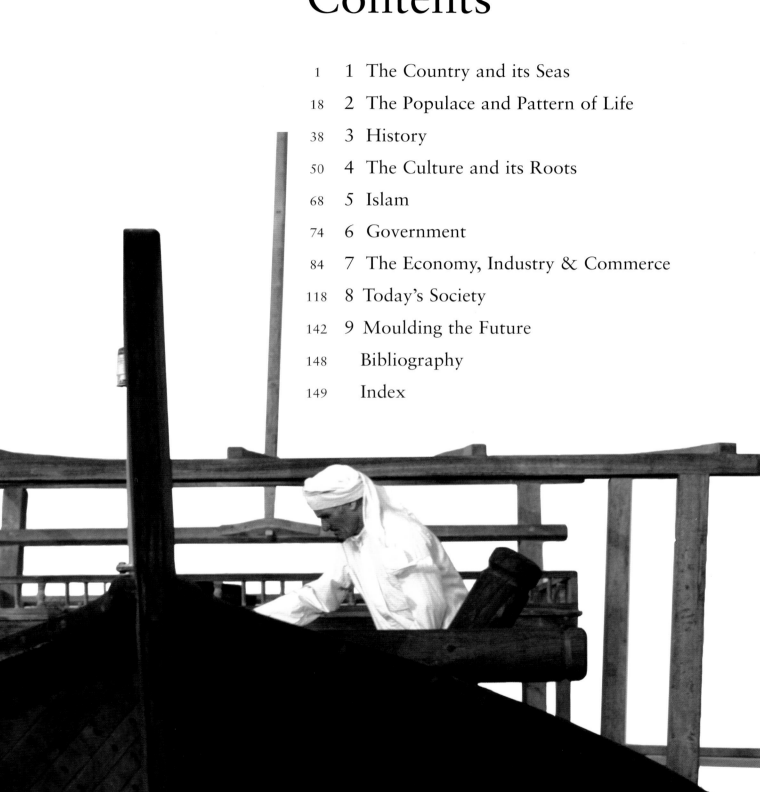

# STATE OF QATAR

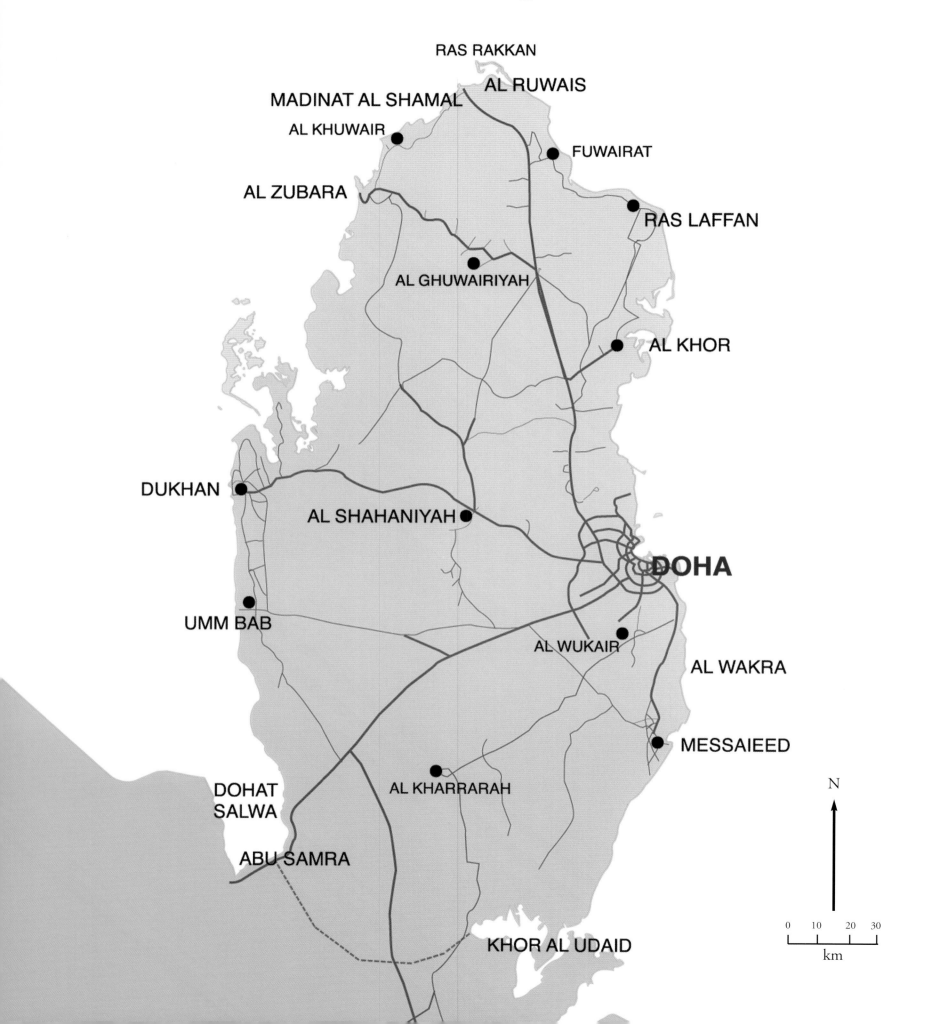

# 1 The Country and its Seas

The peninsula of Qatar projects northwards midway along the western coast of the Arabian mainland into the Arabian Gulf. The total length of the land is approximately 180 kilometres, or 111 miles, and its greatest width along its east-west axis is about 85 km. The state includes a number of islands: Al

To the visitors, jetting into Doha Airport from all quarters of the globe, the first impression of the Qatar mainland is of an overwhelmingly flat terrain, dun in colour where the sand dunes and loess lie and creamy-white along the low coastal limestone hills – the *jebel*. Bright patches of green mark

landscape are surely the majestic sand-dunes of the south. South of Messaieed the level gravelly plains of the centre and the coastal salt-flats – *sabkhah* – give way abruptly to great rolling folds of fine golden sand. Some are crescent-shaped, others form long ridges with wind-scalloped crests, dune melting into

Qatar's capital city of Doha, sited on the curve of its broad bay, exemplifies the country's intimacy with its surrounding seas.

Ashat, Sharouh, Al Saffliyah, Al Aliyah, Halul and Ras Rakkan (on the north coast).

Qatar's coastline, including the islands, is over 700 km, approximately 23 per cent of the total coastline of the Gulf. The country lies on a similar latitude to southern Florida and Taiwan. At 50º 45' to 51º 40' east it lies on the same longitude as the Caspian Sea, the tip of the Horn of Africa and some of the Seychelles islands.

modern alfalfa and vegetable farms and the date-palm gardens. Yet once on the ground, the earlier impression of flatness is at once countered by striking variations in the form of the landscape. Even the smallest rise stands out against the low relief of the surrounding terrain, and Qatar's highest point, a 103-metre elevation near Tuwayyir al Hamir in the south-west, assumes the form of a sizeable hill.

The most striking features of the country's

dune. Just as the dunes change their shape year by year by the activity of the wind, so the colours subtly change during the day. In the strong morning sunlight the gold is bleached almost white and distances become deceptive; in the late afternoon the dunes are beautiful, with long bluish-purple shadows emphasising every gentle curve of the sand. Driven by the prevailing northerly winds, the famous *shamal*, the dunes march relentlessly down to

The sea has for century upon century provided Qatar with its sources of livelihood – its fish, its pearls, and more lately its seabed hydrocarbons.

Khor Al Udaid, known in English as the Inland Sea. This is an irregularly-shaped tidal lagoon, about 25 km. in length, separating Qatar from Saudi Arabia.

Like the Arabian Gulf itself, the Inland Sea is a drowned estuary. Twenty thousand years ago, during the last Ice Age, the river itself flowed from the Asir Mountains and the Yemen highlands of southwest Arabia to join with the combined waters of the rivers Tigris and Euphrates. On the hills to the south of the lagoon lies a band of river gravel, composed of fragments of quartz, granite and slate, 60 metres above sea-level – the remains of an ancient Arabian landscape. Today's Inland Sea is all that is left of the long-vanished river. The strong tidal movement is enough to prevent the narrow entrance from silting up and

isolating the lagoon from the Gulf, but one day it will disappear altogether. The belt of sand-dunes drifts steadily south in front of the wind, and the desert sands are gradually filling the lagoon.

Since the advent of the 4-wheel-drive vehicle the sand-dunes have provided a weekend venue for adventurous desert driving, popular with both Qataris and expatriates. Desert drivers are also drawn to a group of large, isolated crescent dunes in the centre of Qatar, south of the road that runs from Doha to Abu Samrah on the border with Saudi Arabia. These are the celebrated 'singing dunes', where the shape of the individual grains of sand produces a low, reverberating, booming roar when the sand is moved by human disturbance – on the larger scale. Individual footsteps produce a squeaking

sound. This rare and fascinating characteristic is not shared by the dunes further south.

Qatar's land area can be seen as separating into three distinct regions: the sand-dunes of the south, the low-lying coastline with its extensive salt-flats, and the limestone plateau of the Qatari hinterland. In the west, around Dukhan and on the small peninsula of Al Abruq, are *mesas*: small plateaux and free-standing mushroom-shaped pillars of gleaming white limestone, their sides hollowed by the wind so that their tops overhang their foundations. The stone and clays of which these spectacular formations are composed contain many fossils of shells, corals and echinoderms (sea-urchins). These formations were laid down during the Miocene era about 24 million years ago, a period of rich marine life. The harder layer that protects them, composed of sand and gravel, is known as the 'Hofuf formation'.

Some five million years ago a layer of gravel was washed over much of Qatar's landmass by the river flowing from western Arabia, to which we have already referred. Consequently the ground surface is covered with a variety of geological specimens, in the form of smooth pebbles and rocks, whose origin lies many hundreds of miles from Qatar. Some are rolled and polished by the wind to form the curious three-sided shapes known as 'dreikanters'.

The presence of fossilised sea-creatures makes it apparent that Qatar's sedimentary rocks, which dominate the landmass, must once have originated beneath the waters of the Arabian Gulf. In fact the oldest visible rocks are limestones containing salt deposits, dating back about 55 million years to the Eocene era. They are known as the 'Rus' formation and occur in the centre of the country, where they form grey-coloured, wind-scarred rocky pavements, in the core of the eroded Dukhan anti-cline on the west coast, and along the border to the south. Salts within the 'Rus' limestone precipitate as gypsum, traditionally used in Qatar as carved decoration for facing important buildings, and calcium sulphate (anhydrite). It is also a source of the rock-salt which at one time was collected by the bedouin people in south-west Qatar.

During the Pleistocene period, beginning around two million years ago, successive Ice Ages confined much of the earth's water to the ice caps, resulting in a global drop in sea levels. From the last interglacial period about 120,000 years ago the world's climate became increasingly colder, reaching a nadir around 20,000 years ago. The shallow depression forming the Arabian Gulf is estimated to have been above sea-level between 70,000 and 44,000 years ago. The sea then gradually entered the Gulf, only to recede and leave it dry again by about 15,000 years ago. Sand dried out and formed dunes, and soil from the bed of the Gulf blew onto the landmass that is now Qatar, forming the thin topsoil and loess that supports the desert vegetation today. The sea returned once more, but the sea-levels have continued to fluctuate: evidence from the last 8,000 years reveals differences of up to two metres in mean sea-level. During the period between 7,000 and 4,000 years ago high tide reached as much as two metres above today's level, which is why ancient sea-shore fishing settlements are found as much as a kilometre inland from the present coast. The sea then

Salty mud flats – *sabkhah,(above left)* are a feature of much of the coastline of the Gulf. The more complex sea swamps of part of the Qatari littoral *(above right)* are intimidating to man, but a haven for marine and bird life.

receded and rose once more in the second millenium BC, before falling again.

While the nomadic way of life has been all but superseded in today's Qatar, members of the traditionally bedouin communities, straddling the Saudi border, continue to maintain herds of camels and sheep, which graze the sparse scrub of the hinterland. The animal owners and their families will as a rule be resident in the towns, and able to manage their herds and flocks with the help of four-wheel-drive vehicles and herders.

The easing of pressure on domestic grazing has allowed successive governments both to assist in the preservation of existing wildlife and to restore or re-introduce important species that were previously under threat.

The indomitable mangroves (*above*) of the coast provide a source of durable wood for man's buildings and tools.

Significant stretches of inland Qatar, particularly in the south, are comprised of vertebral ridges (*left*) which advance annually by the movement of wind.

The surveying and mapping of Qatar's desert region (*right*) is a continuous process.

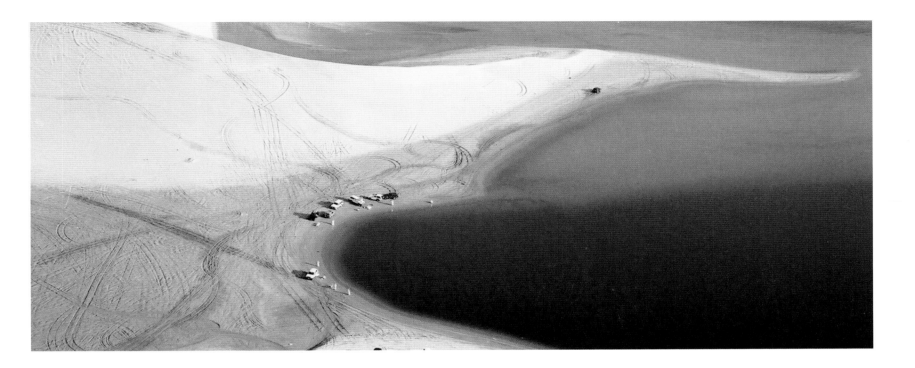

In the region of the so-called Inland Sea (Khor Al Udaid) in the south-east of the peninsula, the pure sand sweeps up to form characteristic crescent-shaped *barchan*.

*Below: Mesas* of harder rock defy erosion of the wind and leave behind vast mushroom-shaped monuments.

## Ecological and Conservation Programmes

Until the 1940s and '50s, the Arabian white oryx, *Oryx leucoryx,* roamed Arabia's Empty Quarter, Rub Al Khali. A combination of harsh conditions and over-eager hunters brought the species to the brink of extinction. Qatar recognised the looming disaster relatively early. From the start of the 1960s, it began to build up several breeding herds of Arabian oryx. One herd, bred from pairs given by a former education minister, Sheikh Jassem Bin Hamad Al Thani, is currently located in Al Shahaniyah. A huge new reserve is being established in the north west of the peninsula for *Leucoryx*, Reem gazelle and other deer. Both are managed by the country's Ministry of Municipal Affairs and Agriculture. Other protected herds are maintained on private farms, notably by the Prime Minister, Sheikh Abdullah Bin Khalifa Al Thani.

*Oryx leucoryx,* with its two long annulated horns, is the creature which some say gave rise to the legend of the unicorn. In profile, the horns appear as one. Known locally as *m'hat* or *al wodhi* (the clear), the oryx's prime habitat was the southeastern part of Rub Al Khali bordering on Oman. A gregarious antelope, the oryx in the wild will cover anything up to 25 kilometres a night, browsing and grazing the sparse desert vegetation. Its dark splayed hooves, with a characteristic white band, make movement across the soft sands easy. Front hooves are used to scoop out shallow depressions, in which to rest in the shade of acacia trees during the intense heat of mid-day.

Oryx have a life span of around 25 years. A full-grown adult stands 90-120 centimetres at the shoulder, and weighs on average between 100 and 150kg. The horns, which grow to a length of around 70-75 centimetres, are used for self defence against natural enemies such as the desert wolf, but the fiercely protective male oryx or ox will also use his horns to ward off young calves which approach the ewes during the mating season. *Leucoryx* is remarkably adapted to the harsh desert environment; it can go for long periods without drinking and can tolerate dehydration of up to 20 per cent of its body weight. The light coat is believed to reflect solar radiation, helping the animal cope with temperatures which can climb to over 50° Celsius. Temperatures inland can fall dramatically at night and in the winter, when the bedouin say the darker hair on its legs allow the oryx to absorb warmth retained from the desert sands.

At birth, the calf has a greyish coat which takes on a light brown hue as it gets older, gradually changing to a creamy white, tinged with reddish brown, and the characteristic colouring of the adult.

The strongest male leads the herd, and is the only one to mate with the females. His supremacy is often challenged by younger males. If flight is impossible, a leading male will move to the front of the herd, standing with its head down and its horns pointing towards an attacker. The horns of a charging oryx can pierce the wood of a heavy door, which indicates the damage it can do to another animal!

Qatar's growing herds provide the hope that, like the Reem Gazelle these creatures may successfully be re-introduced to the wild in a society which now understands the need for conservation.

Not as tall as the oryx and much lighter, the *Reem Gazelles* (otherwise known as Arabian Gazelles or *Gazella subgotturosa*) are also natives of the Arabian peninsula. In Qatar they are extinct in the wild, but preserved in wide ranging captivity. The young can run almost as swiftly as their elders within days of birth, and depend on their mother's milk for only the first eight weeks. An adult Reem can grow to 90 or 120 centimetres and weigh between 30 and 40kg. The males generally have longer curved and slightly flattened horns than the females, the horns sometimes reaching a length of 25 centimetres. In addition to the animals in Doha's zoo and being bred on private farms or the government reserve, Ras Laffan Industrial City's Environmental Section introduced a 15-strong herd to the area in March 1999. Their growth, feeding habits and breeding patterns are monitored in a 55,000 square mile reserve (*14.26 million hectares*). To supplement their natural grazing, the Reem are fed on a diet of *barseem* grass and pellets containing cereal, grains, vegetable proteins, molasses, salt and mineral supplements. They are also checked for parasites.

Proving that environmental awareness and industrial development can exist side by side, Ras Laffan has also developed a mangrove conservation programme, recording data on the flora and fauna, protecting the turtle nesting beaches and re-introducing the Ostrich (*Struthio camelius*), last spotted in the wild on the Arabian peninsula in 1941. In conjunction with various other organisations in Qatar, Ras Laffan has produced booklets identifying the plants, birds and other wildlife found naturally in the area (including the Spiny-Tailed Lizard, *Uromastix microlepis* and the Monitor Lizard, *Varanus griseus*). It has also introduced a programme to 'rescue' and 'rehabilitate' sea snakes (*Hydrophis lapemoides* and *Hydrophis cyanocinctus*). From time to time luckless sea snakes are sucked into the water intake used for cooling purposes in the industrial city.

The Arabian oryx – once on the brink of extinction – now flourishes as a herd in the Al Shahaniya region of central Qatar, under a skilfully managed and monitored programme of mammal conservation.

## Other Fauna ... and Flora

Although bordering on eastern Saudi Arabia, Qatar supports a fauna and flora which differs significantly from that country.

As a rule, human occupation of previously uninhabited land is seen as having a negative impact on wild life, but in Qatar the reverse is true. Until the beginning of the 'oil era' there was no open surface water in Qatar; now effluent drainage ponds with thick beds of reeds (*Australis phragmites*) near Doha and Messaieed provide a haven for many resident breeding birds and the thousands of migrants which pass through Qatar twice a year. Gardens and parks in towns and villages attract birds and insects.

## Mammals

Land mammals in Qatar are mainly nocturnal, although Cape Hares (*Lepus capensis*) and foxes can be seen during the day in the cooler months. Many desert mammals are smaller and lighter versions of their European relatives, with specialised adaptations to enable them to survive in a harsh, arid environment. Foxes, hedgehogs, hares, wild cats and jerboas all have large ears to assist with heat loss; the blood circulating through the fine capillaries is cooled by the breeze. Tufts of hair between the pads of their feet give a grip on soft sand and offer some protection during the hotter months. Desert species tend to be lighter-coloured than those of darker habitats.

Hares are distributed all over the country. The Cape Hare is a smaller version of its European cousin, and its soft greyish-brown fur provides perfect camouflage. The animal relies on this for protection, remaining motionless when danger threatens and only running at the last moment. During the heat of the day hares shelter in shallow, excavated depressions in the side of the wind-blown sandy hummocks which form beside clumps of vegetation. They breed during the cooler months, producing two young.

The hare's only natural enemy is the fox. The Arabian Red Fox (*Vulpes vulpes arabica*) is widespread throughout the country but is rarely sighted except around the coastal *jebel* in the north-east and north-west. Like the European fox, the Arabian fox will adapt to living alongside man, haunting the outskirts of farms and gardens. It is an opportunistic hunter, eating anything it can catch and also desert fruits and plants.

In the far south of Qatar lives a rare and much smaller, strictly nocturnal fox, the Ruppell's Sand Fox (*Vulpes ruppelli*). Weighing

only 1.5 kilos, it has large ears, a bushy, white-tipped tail and golden-brown eyes. The Sand Fox cannot coexist with the Red Fox, which would undoubtedly hunt it for prey. It is never found near human settlement, preferring the remoteness of the dunes.

The Ethiopian Hedgehog (*Parachinus aethiopicus*) is widely distributed in Qatar and adapts easily to living in cultivated land and near human habitation. It is common around the farms on the outskirts of Doha and on the estates at Shahaniya. Light brown with white-tipped spines, it has a bald patch on the top of its head. The face is black or dark grey with a surrounding lighter area. It can be seen at dusk emerging from its burrow to hunt for insects, grubs, wild fruits and small reptiles, and will attack poisonous snakes without fear. Hedgehogs breed in May-June, producing up to six young. It is highly likely that the Long-eared Hedgehog (*Hemiechinus auritus*) also occurs in Qatar, although it has not yet been officially recorded.

The rare and shy little Sand Cat (*Felis margarita*) was twice recorded in Qatar in the late 1980s, in an area bordering on Saudi Arabia. It is a delicate-looking animal, orange-brown with a white underside, white feet, large black-tipped ears and black-striped front legs. Exclusively nocturnal, it digs a burrow, emerging in the evening to hunt for rodents, reptiles and insects.

Three species of desert-living rodent are represented in Qatar. They form the prey of foxes, monitor lizards, raptors and owls. The Lesser Jerboa (*Jaculus jaculus vocator*) prefers desert bordering on gravel plains rather than deep sand. Jerboas have enlarged hind legs and move by hopping, often making leaps of as much as a metre. The long tail has a flat tuft at the end, which assists the animal in keeping its balance as it jumps and also acts as a 'prop' when the jerboa sits up on its hind legs, hence its nickname of 'kangaroo mouse'. It is sandy in colour with a white belly and large ears, and being predominantly nocturnal it has

The weathering of limestone has produced this dramatic leonine formation on the Al Abruq peninsula of western Qatar.

An unexpected basin *(right)* in the Jebel Al Jusasiyah hides a rare lake, whose water is brackish.

Qatar's largest cave, Dahl Al Misfir, *(below)* is not only an attraction to visitors but home to a colony of bats.

conspicuously large eyes. Jerboas survive without drinking, deriving their moisture from plants and dew. Gerbils are represented by two species: the Arabian Gerbil (*Gerbillus nanus arabium*) and the Cheesman's Gerbil (*Gerbillus cheesmani cheesmani*). The latter is widespread throughout the country and numerically the most abundant mammal. The animals are similar in appearance, with pointed snouts, chestnut-brown bodies, white bellies and long tails. The coat of the Arabian Gerbil is darker. Unlike the jerboa, it runs on four legs, but is capable of leaping considerable distances. In the hottest period of summer some rodents aestivate in deep burrows, the equivalent of hibernation in colder countries.

Two species of bat are found in Qatar: the Trident Leaf-nosed Bat (*Asellia tridens tridens*) and Hemprich's Long-eared Bat (*Otonycteris hemprichi*). The Leaf-nosed Bat occurs all over the Arabian peninsula, and in Qatar it inhabits the large cave near the Salwa Road known as Dahl al Misfir and another cave, partly filled with water, on the northern outskirts of Doha. It is also found in ruins and old-established date-palm groves. The Long-eared Bat is larger, with a slower flight, and is less common.

Dolphins are frequently seen in Qatari waters and can be observed from beaches and

even from the Doha Corniche. At least four species are represented, and one species of porpoise. Common Dolphins (*Delphinus delphis*) prefer the deeper water offshore, and will form schools of up to a hundred. The animal is dark grey with yellow and light grey markings. Inshore, a type of dolphin, *Tursiops aduncus,* very similar to the universally-known Bottlenose Dolphin (*Tursiops truncatus*) is more often seen. The Humpback Dolphin (*Sousa chinensis*), a shy animal forming smaller groups than the Common Dolphin, and the Rough-toothed Dolphin *(Steno bredanensis)* are sometimes seen offshore. Very rare is the Black Finless Porpoise (*Neophocaena phocaenoides*), an animal superficially resembling a dolphin but with a blunt head and lacking a dorsal fin.

Whales rarely enter Qatari waters as they prefer to inhabit deeper water than occurs in the Gulf, but may occasionally take refuge in the calmer seas from storms in the Indian Ocean. Occasional appearances of the Bryde's Whale (*Balaenoptera edeni*), a baleen whale

feeding on small shoaling fish, are reported by fishermen and dead specimens sometimes wash up on beaches. A very large Bryde's Whale, measuring 12 metres in length, was caught near Doha in 1958.

The Arabian Gulf is home to the second largest population of Dugongs (*Dugong dugong*) in the world, probably numbering about 5,000. Their main concentration is in the coastal waters of western Abu Dhabi, but they are seen from time to time off Qatar. World wide the population has decreased rapidly, due to hunting and other causes, and the Arabian Gulf, where they are protected, may be the dugongs' last hope of survival. An adult male dugong measures nearly 3 metres in length. Dugongs feed on sea-grasses, surfacing occasionally to breathe. Unlike dolphins and whales they never leap from the water but are slow-moving, placid animals, although they can move fast when alarmed. Within the last decade a herd of dugongs numbering several hundred was sighted just north of the Qatar mainland.

As tradition requires, herds of camels (*above and opposite*) still browse the desert scrub, and are valued for their meat, milk, leather and fur, even if their keepers are now living a settled, rather than a bedouin, life.

Scrub desert supports herds of hardy sheep (*right*)

The delicate Reem, or Arabian gazelle, is once again on the increase in Qatar, in a 55,000 square miles (14.24 million hectares) reserve near Ras Laffan (*above*). Vulnerable calves sometimes need the intervention of human nursing (*left*).

## Birds

Besides being home to birds which reside in Qatar all year, frequenting parks and gardens as well as the desert and the coast, Qatar provides a vital resting location during the autumn and spring migrations, when thousands of birds pass through the country. Undoubtedly farms, gardens and surface water areas, which include (purified) effluent ponds and the lakes on the golf course in the West Bay area of Doha, contribute greatly to their survival, and the number of species recorded in the country increases year by year.

Coastal birds include Black-winged Stilts, Terns, Gulls, Turnstones, Sanderlings, Kentish Plovers, Common and Spotted Redshanks and Greenshanks. The golf course, with its wide variety of trees and shrubs and stretches of open water, attracts water-fowl such as Coot, Ducks and Geese. Shrikes of several species frequent the area, preying on smaller birds, insects and rodents.

The area of natural mangrove forest in Khor Shaqiq bay, near Al Dakhira, and the more recently planted mangrove areas around the mainland coast and on the islands, provide a haven for many species. Both the Common and Smyrna Kingfisher are seen here, and Western Reef and Grey Herons and Egrets nest in the trees. Pallid Harriers and Kestrels quarter the area for prey. The Osprey, a large, fish-eating raptor resembling an eagle, is well represented in Qatar and will frequent coastal towns as well as open coastline. The Inland Sea (Khor Al Udaid) and the stretch of coast immediately north of Doha attract large populations of long-legged, pink Greater Flamingoes.

Desert birds include several species of Larks and Wheatears and the secretive Stone Curlew.

The 'Inland Sea' at Khor Al Udaid and Doha's local coasts are home to the greater flamingo (*above*). The Arabian bustard (*left*) is a regular visitor to Qatar. Most familiar of the raptors circling the skies is the kestrel (*right*).

Houbara Bustard are hunted in season with falcons. A certain sign of hot weather approaching is the arrival in Qatar of two species of migrating Bee-eaters: the brilliantly coloured European Bee-eater and the Little Green Bee-eater. They rest and hunt insects for a few days before heading north.

Comparatively recent arrivals include the grey and black Indian House Crow, now resident along one stretch of the north-east coast, and the Common Mynah, whose numbers have rapidly increased since the 1990s. Raucous colonies of the latter inhabit the palm-trees along Doha's Corniche. Another noisy city-dweller is the Rose-ringed Parakeet, a big green parakeet which may have originated from escaped cage-birds imported from India. They congregate at sunset in leafy trees and on the top of tall lighting poles in Doha.

### Reptiles

Qatar has a wide variety of lizards and a smaller number of snakes. The poisonous land snakes are members of the viper family, whereas sea snakes are related to cobras. The Horned Viper (*Cerastes cerastes gasperetti*) is widespread in desert areas but is rarely seen, being nocturnal. It is not aggressive, but its habit of burying itself in sand makes it potentially dangerous if accidentally stepped on. It will sometimes move over loose sand-surfaces, such as dunes, by sidewinding, a serpentine movement where only two points of the snake's body are in contact with the ground at one time. This leaves curious tracks in the shape of a repeated elongated 's'. In former years the bedouin reported sightings of the very dangerous and aggressive Carpet or Saw-Scaled Viper (*Echis carinatus*) and Burton's

Carpet Viper (*Echis coloratus*) within the southern border of Qatar, but these have not yet been officially recorded.

Non-poisonous snakes include the Rat Snake (*Coluber ventromaculatus*), a long grey-brown snake which is active during the day, sometimes climbing trees to prey on birds' eggs and nestlings. It is seen in gardens and on open ground within Doha and other urban areas, and will frequent stone walls such as those of the old town of Zubara on the north-west coast. The Sand Snake (*Psammophis schokari*) is also active by day and is found in cultivated areas and gardens as well as open desert. An elegant, fast-moving reptile with black and white streaks on a grey-brown body, it attains a maximum 155 cms in length and is Qatar's longest snake.

The Leaf-nosed snake (*Lytorhynchus diadema*) is a much smaller nocturnal reptile found only in sandy or stony habitats; it gets its name from its distinctive wedge-shaped snout. the Arabian sand boa (*Eryx jayakari*) is particularly well adapted to its environment, eyes and nostrils placed well up on the head so that it can bury itself in the sand and await its victims.

Five species of sea snake inhabit Qatari waters. Their venom is even more deadly than that of the cobras to which they are related, but they are not aggressive to humans and there are no recently recorded cases of sea snake bite. The Yellow-bellied Sea Snake (*Pelamis platurus*) is a large dark-brown snake with a pale underside; the body is flattened, belt-like. It is encountered far out at sea, feeding on pelagic fish. Inshore, more commonly seen reptiles are the Arabian Gulf Sea Snake (*Hydrophis lapemoides*) and the Blue Sea Snake (*Hydrophis cyanocinctus*), both large creamy-green snakes banded with grey. The

Examples of Qatar's wildlife include, anticlockwise from the top of the page, the Spiny-tailed *dhub* (which takes in all its moisture from the air), the Arabian Sand Boa, the Desert Hare, the Ethiopian Hedgehog, and the Red Fox.

Common Sea-Snake (*Enhydra schistosa*), banded with charcoal-grey, is also found inshore.

Lizards represent the largest section of Qatar's reptiles. One that is often seen crossing desert roads is the large Spiny-tailed Lizard (*Uromastyx uromastyx*) known as '*dhub*' in Arabic. It has a heavy spiked tail and sharp claws but is a harmless vegetarian, living in burrows in colonies all over the country. It is regarded as a gastronomic delicacy by desert-dwellers. The largest lizard is the Desert Monitor (*Varanus grisieus*) called *wirral* in Arabic. It is a carnivorous hunter and eater of carrion and inhabits the central gravel plain. All the other species of lizard are insect-eaters. They include the Toad-head Agama (*Phrenocephalus arabicus*), the glossy, beautifully marked Sand Skink (*Scinus mitranus*) and its relative the Garden Skink (*Chalcides ocellatus*). Yellow-bellied House Geckos (*Hemidactylus flaviviridus*) are found in houses and on garden walls throughout Qatar.

Turtles were once far more numerous in the Arabian Gulf than they are today. The giant Leatherback Turtle (*Dermochelys coriacea*) has not been recorded off Qatar since 1979. Four species survive. Hawksbill and Green Turtles still nest on islands and on one mainland site. The Hawksbill (*Eretmochelys imbricata*) has an amber-coloured shell with dark markings and overlapping scutes; the animal's projecting beak gives it its name. The Green Turtle (*Chelonia mydas*) is larger and can reach a maximum weight of 150 kilos. An occasional visitor is the Olive Ridley (*Lepidochelys olivacea*), a small turtle weighing only 50 kilos. The Loggerhead Turtle (*Caretta caretta*) prefers deep water and rarely comes inshore.

## Insects and other Arthropods

The desert habitat of Qatar supports a surprisingly wide variety of insect life. Thirteen orders of insects are represented, with numerous species in most groups. These include butterflies, moths, beetles, dragonflies, crickets, bees, wasps and mantises.

The inhabitants of urban areas, where orange and lemon trees are grown, are familiar with the spectacular black and yellow Citrus Swallowtail butterfly (*Papilio demoleus*). Other garden species include the ground-hatching Arabian Cicada (*Platypleura arabica*); the loud continuous shrilling of the male insects is a familiar sound from May onwards. Taking over from them at night are the crickets, including the chirruping House Cricket (*Acheta domestica*), found in almost every home.

Desert beetles include the Domino Beetle

The desert scrub is home to a wide range of insects including those pictured here: from the top, the Domino beetle, the Fat-tailed scorpion, the Praying mantis, the Towerhead grasshopper and the Orb spider.

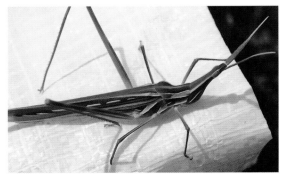

The Painted Lady is by far the most widely distributed of the world's butterflies. A strong migrant, it may suddenly occur in numbers in habitats where it cannot survive on a permanent basis.

The Royal Angelfish *(Pygoplites diacanthus),* with its brilliant colours, is a common sight among the reefs of the Gulf

*(Anthia duodeciguttata),* black with a dozen splashy white spots and instantly recognisable as it emerges at dusk to hunt other insects. Areas where camels are kept are frequented by big, shiny black Scarab Beetles of which the most common is *Scarabeus cristatus.* They trundle balls of dung around before burying them, each containing a single egg. Anywhere with vegetation has a population of Pitted Beetles *(Adesmia cancellata),* small and black and resembling a sunflower seed, which ambles across the desert floor on long legs and feeds off organic debris from plants. Small funnel-shaped pits in the sand are the work of Antlions *(Myrmeleontides),* a numerous species whose voracious larvae construct these pits, then hide at the bottom and bombard any passing ant with grains of sand until it falls. Other relentless hunters are the praying mantises, of which many species are present in Qatar.

Scorpions are plentiful in the desert, sheltering during the day under rocks and pieces of wood and in the burrows of lizards. At least two kinds of scorpion inhabit Qatar. The black, Fat-tailed Scorpion *(Androctonus crassicauda)* can reach up to 12 cms in length, but its sting is less poisonous than that of a smaller, yellow-green species. The venom of scorpions attacks the nervous system.

Spiders range from very large and active nocturnal ground hunting spiders, which measure as much as 11 cms across, down to tiny coloured crab spiders which hide in flowers to grab their prey. Delicate, beautifully patterned web-spinning Orb spiders *(Argiopidae)* string their webs on Zygophyllum shrubs in the depressions; they are sometimes called Signature spiders from their habit of weaving a zig-zag line across the web.

Fast-moving and extraordinary-looking arachnids are the large and hairy so-called Camel Spiders *(Solifugidae)* which are not as common in Qatar as in the wadis of the UAE.

### Marine Life

The Marine Aquarium at Qatar National Museum gives an excellent introduction to the wealth of the country's marine life.

Demersal fish, inhabiting the sea-bed, number some 150 species, most of them commercially valuable. They include Emperors, Jacks, Sweetlips, Groupers, Snappers and Barracudas. Other commercially valuable species include Shrimps, Slipper Lobsters, Squid and Cuttlefish. Pelagic species include five species of Shark and Mackerel, Tuna, Herring and Sardines. Major fishing ports are Doha, Al Khor and Al Ruwais. The richest fishing grounds are all to the north-east of the mainland.

The Gulf waters are among some of the most saline in the world, and the water is not clear enough for massive coral growths. However, a number of corals do grow in the Gulf and Qatar has a number of small reefs. Except for an area off Fuwairat in the north-east and another at the entrance to the Inland Sea (Khor Al Udaid), most are found offshore around the islands. In depths of between 6 and 12 metres, growths of staghorn, star, brain and table coral attract colourful Parrotfish which feed on the coral itself, and anenome-dwelling orange and white little Clown fish, fiercely protective of their homes. There are Starry Puffer fish, Surgeon fish with barbed stings, and graceful Lion fish with their feathery but deadly stings. Leopard Rays and Common Sting-rays often stay close to reefs. Other inhabitants are the short and long spined Sea Urchins, crabs of many kinds, Sea Cucumbers and the strange, colourful Nudibranchs, or Sea Slugs.

Sharks are plentiful in Qatari waters, and are not known to attack humans, although in the old pearl-fishing days, when boats anchored for weeks at a time and sharks overcame their natural caution, they would harass divers. Sting-rays can inflict painful but non-lethal stings. The trailing tentacles of jellyfish can leave long-lasting scars on the skin of the unwary swimmer. The most dangerous fish is the deadly Stone-fish, which so closely resembles a weed-covered rock that it is difficult to detect even in a close-up photograph. A victim of Stone-fish venom treated at Hamad Hospital a few years ago required two weeks of intensive care.

### Natural Vegetation

The key factors which affect plant growth in Qatar are high temperatures and low rainfall, together with the high salinity of the soil and groundwater. Plants have evolved various strategies to survive.

Most desert plants have their growing period during late autumn, winter and spring, to take advantage of the cooler weather and whatever rainfall there may be. However, low rainfall in recent years has meant that plants have had to rely for water entirely on the condensation at night. Seeds of annuals may lie dormant for years, awaiting sufficient moisture for germination. Of late, most flowering plants have been perennials, with roots delving deep into the ground. The bedouin divide plants into *ussh* – annuals – that grow and flower after rain

– and *shajar*, namely the perennial plants and trees that survive the heat of summer.

The most prolifically growing trees in Qatar are acacias. The most widespread is *Acacia tortilis*, a salt-tolerant tree with small leaves to reduce evaporation and sharp thorns as protection against grazing animals. Another dense, thorn-spiked tree of the depressions known as *rawdhats*, where moisture collects, is *Ziziphus nummularia*. Most desert trees have to defend themselves against camels, goats and sheep either with sharp spikes or by growing beyond the animals' reach, as is the case with the *Ghaf* trees (*prosopis cineraria*). These gnarled, ancient-looking trees may well be hundreds of years old; traditionally they were a source of firewood, fodder and edible fruits for the bedouin.

Both annual and perennial plants tend to grow close to the ground, where the heat reflected from the soil and rock may be 20-30ºc. higher than the atmospheric temperature. Consequently, plants guard against dessication by developing small leaves or in some cases few or none. Others have leaves with tough cuticles, or that roll up to reduce exposure to the wind.

The mangroves (*Avicennia marina*) of the east coast have adapted to one of the most extreme environments for any plant, highly saline water, by excreting the salt as crystals on their dark-green leathery leaves. The trees are smaller than mangroves in other regions because of the extra energy required for this process. Aerial roots called pneumatophores protrude above the sea-saturated silt to enable the trees to breathe. Mangroves provide an important habitat for birds, insects, fish and marine invertebrates.

In the winter, along the saline flats beside the mangrove forests grows a parasite that feeds on salt-tolerant plants, the bright yellow and maroon spikes of the Desert Hyacinth (*Cistanche tubulosa*), a member of the Broomrape family. It usually attaches its long, horizontal root to tap into those of *Limonium axillare*, a plant with delicate dry sprays of small purple flowers, or of *Zygophyllum qatarense*, a small shrub with purplish fleshy, globular leaves. Another parasite is the aptly-named Red Thumb (*Cynomorium coccineum*) which used to be eaten by the bedouin.

Many kinds of grass survive intensive grazing and will grow tall and thick, given rain. Even in the driest spring the long, trailing stems of the Desert Squash (*Citrillus colocynthis*) can be seen in the depressions, bearing green and yellow fruits the size of tennis balls – alas, bitter and inedible.

The *ghaf* tree *(prosopis cineraria)* provides deep shade, and can live for hundreds of years.

The Desert Hyacinth *(above and right)* blooms brightly after a splash of rain; the Red Thumb *(below, right)*, and the Opuntia Cactus *(below)* can survive the fierce heat of summer.

# 2 The Populace and Pattern of Life

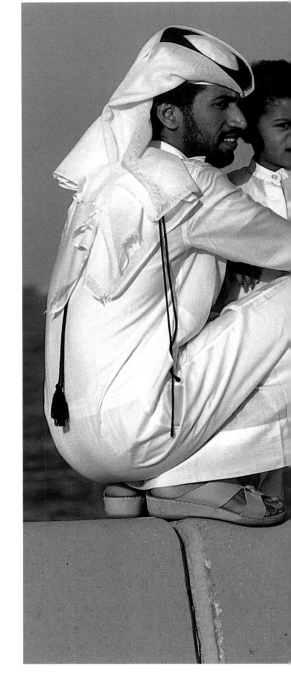

The process of industrialisation and development has taken hundreds of years in many countries, but Qatar has changed from a quiet and little known community of nomads and fishermen to become one of the world's major clean energy suppliers commanding international respect in little over 50 years – less than a single lifetime. The changes have been dramatic and enormous, but the country has achieved the transformation with a unique blend of traditional and modern reflected in everything from its architecture to the lifestyle of its people.

Although Qatar's population, totalling some 700,000, is concentrated in and around Doha, the business and administrative capital, there are several other important towns and villages. Qatar's industrial cities in the northeast, southeast and west are developing their own extensive residential and commercial areas, and the excellent road network with extensive dual carriageways makes journeys short, encouraging more people to settle either in the suburbs or outside the capital area. Nevertheless, according to the 1997 figures, 264,009 people lived in Doha, and a further 169,774 in Al Rayyan municipality – nowadays part of the capital's conurbation.

Qatari nationals are employed both in the government and private sectors, and with great emphasis on the development of the educational system, both men and women are being trained in new skills and for new professions, reducing the country's dependence on its multinational expatriate community.

The standard of living is high and most nationals as well as many expatriates enjoy the benefits of a high disposable income. Although there is a twelve-route bus network, most people rely on their own cars, taxis, or motor vehicle transport to and from work provided by their employers. Over 270,000 vehicles were registered in 1998, with some 20,000 new – but not necessarily additional – vehicles registered each year. Women are permitted to drive, but most Qatari and some expatriate families will employ a driver and set aside a vehicle specifically for the women and children in the family. A high percentage of middle to upper income families of all nationalities employ at least part time domestic help, as cooks, nannies, gardeners and for general household duties.

Among Qataris, family values remain at the core of everyday life. Activities are designed with families in mind and shops and leisure facilities

The Corniche in Doha is a popular location for families taking the air.

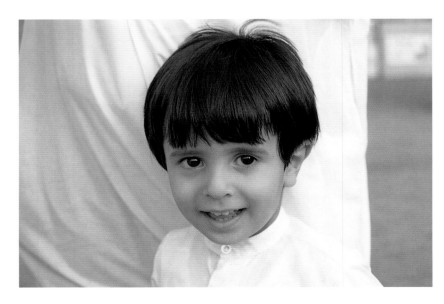

A bright future awaits Qatar's coming generation.

18

offer 'ladies only' or 'family only' days or times. Many of the banks operate special branches solely for female customers. Post Offices and departments such as Immigration and Passport Control, the Traffic Police licencing section, and most customer service departments have similar Ladies Only sections, separate windows to deal with enquiries from women – or allow women to by-pass the queueing structure.

Recently, Qatar introduced a two-day weekend – Friday and Saturday – in the government sector, a move which has spread into the quasi government and private sectors. Bankers maintain a six day week, (Saturday to Thursday). The oil gas and petrochemicals

sector, however, has opted to maximise its contacts with the world markets by closing on Fridays and Saturdays. Many shops continue to open six and a half or seven days a week. A number of private companies offer their employees a five day week, but with rotating shifts to cover Thursdays and Saturdays.

**Doha** (Al Doha) takes its name from the shape of the bay on which it lies half way down the east coast of the peninsula. It has both an international airport and a sea port which has been extended to include a separate container port, large enough to accommodate even visiting aircraft carriers. Many of the government ministries have their headquarters

along the Corniche, a 7 km landscaped dual carriageway and parallel pedestrian area which sweeps round the bay, from the airport to the pyramid-shaped Sheraton Hotel. The Emir's working palace (Diwan Emiri) is half way along the shoreline, close to the dhow harbour and overlooking the small, recreational Palm Island in the centre of the bay. Several parks line the Corniche, providing open-air venues for traditional dancing and community activities at festival times. Al Bida Park, close to the Qatar National Theatre, has two art galleries and an open air theatre as well as extensive water features, and all sorts of children's facilities such as small boats, a ferris wheel and a skateboarding half-pipe. The pedestrianised areas and lawns of the Corniche and parks are used extensively by picnickers and joggers.

Among several other parks, the largest is in the Al Muntaza district. Each suburb or *farij* has its own municipal park, usually with play equipment for the children. Doha's wonderfully designed Zoo, managed by the Ministry of Municipal Affairs and Agriculture, lies on the western outskirts of the city.

Nearby lies the industrial area on the Salwa Road, housing light industries, particularly garment factories, mechanical workshops, food and soft drink processing plants, detergent and furniture manufacturers, carpentry workshops and specialised oil industry support service workshops. A second, adjacent, industrial area is under development nearby. Both will be linked directly to Messaieed Industrial City to the south by a new road which will bypass central Doha.

The old palace complex, at the southern edge of the bay, is now Qatar National Museum. Once it gave directly onto the beach, as suggested today by the position of its lagoon and aquarium. Much of the present Corniche and the whole of the West Bay/Al Dafna area to the west and north of the bay is reclaimed land, right round to the Aladdin's Kingdom Fun Park with its rides, Go-Karts and amusements. Between that and the university campus lies the prestigious new West Bay Lagoon development and the Doha Golf Club. The northern bay area is the site of several new hotel developments including the Ritz Carlton and Inter-Continental.

The once barren sandbank in the centre of Doha bay has been developed and landscaped as Palm Tree Island, a popular playground for the very young.

Doha's shady parks are an excellent venue for picnics.

Doha's green spaces afford a peaceful environment for reading during a break in the working day.

For aspiring footballers, Doha's Corniche provides an early morning jogging route *(right)*. Qatar's record of achievement in sport is outstanding..

Pony rides are a popular pastime for children along the coast *(below)*.

A father conducts his family to savour the cultural heritage in the Ethnographical Museum beneath the wind tower of part of Doha's original Al Thani Palace complex (*below*).

Doha has become a wonderful city for parks and playgrounds. It also boasts several museums. The Qatar National Museum on the Corniche currently houses archaeological, zoological, botanical, geological and ethnographic collections as well as collections of Islamic coins, state medals and awards, costume, traditional medical implements, and an aquarium. Al Koot (Doha fort) preserves collections of weaving and the plastic arts, as well as wood carving. The fort itself has some fine examples of gypsum carving, and each of the rooms surrounding the central courtyard has separate craft displays relating to gypsum burning and carving, rope-making, basketry and wool and cotton carding. Al Koot is not, however, to be confused with the Ethnographical Museum, located in the 'wind tower house' in the centre of town. The Weaponry Museum in the Al Laqta area of Doha has an impressive array of swords, daggers, knives, rifles, pistols, canons and armour dating back to the 16th century. Included are several pure silver or gold *khanjar* (curved daggers) and swords which belonged to the region's rulers. The approximately 2,300 exhibits were bought by the State from the private collection of Sheikh Hassan Bin Mohammed Bin Ali Al Thani in 1994.

A Postal Museum in the old souq area traces the history of the country's postal services and also displays old postal equipment, pillar boxes, and the old hand-written records listing all incoming and outgoing mail by weight of mailbags and places of origin or destination. The Philatelic Bureau in the striking General Post Office in West Bay (a photograph appears on page 121) offers collectors the opportunity to acquire new issues and First Day covers, whilst the Philatelic Club on Al Sadd Street houses the National Stamp Collection.

In the 1950s, Doha was a small town, its houses built around the sandy shore of the bay. With increasing industrialisation and rapid modernisation in the latter part of the twentieth century, many older buildings were replaced – at first by relatively plain two to four storey office, residential and commercial blocks, or single storey villas.

Latterly, land in the centre of the city was at a premium, as taller structures sprang up. At the same time, the style of architecture changed again, with newer villas and multi-storey blocks combining the latest construction materials and techniques with more features of traditional and Islamic architecture. Islamic arches and screens, gypsum features – or glass re-inforced concrete panels featuring gypsum designs – have become

*The Cultural Vision*
Qatar has determinedly set its sights on being the cultural capital of the Gulf. To this end, significant resources are being channeled into related facilities, shown here in artists' visualisations. The Qatar National Library *(top)*, designed by the Japanese architect Arata Isozaki, will dominate the skyline of the Corniche; the new Islamic Museum *(below,*

*right)* at the southern end of the Corniche will house the impressive collection acquired in recent years by the State; the National Museum (shown on page 58) is being refurbished and will include a tunnel leading to a glass viewing room *(below, left)* under the waters of the bay; the innovative technology of the Photographic Museum *(below, bottom)* will alter the angle of the immense shutters to maximise the natural light in the display rooms.

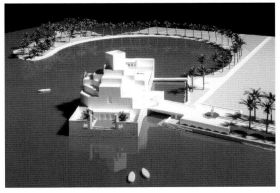

The prestigious Al Dana Club (*left*) offers excellent facilities to its members.

popular, as has the use of coloured aluminium for door and window frames and coloured reflective glass cladding. Qatar's lifestyle reflects the same unique blend of traditional and modern.

The city's fine hotels are invariably landscaped, and usually associated with water. There are private clubs, illustrated on these pages, also giving a seal of grace to today's Doha. Meanwhile the zoological gardens are much more than a source of delight to the younger generation. They help to emphasize an ideological reverance for the natural world. The zoo is divided geographically into sections, for each collection of mammal species – the giraffes and lions, for example, for the African section, tigers for the South Asian. A significant collection covers *genera* from the desert environment to which Qatar itself belongs, including reptiles and insects. It provides a source for zoological research. It lies on the outskirts of the city, close to the Salwa Road Industrial Area and Khalifa Sports City. It is run by the Ministry of Municipal Affairs and Agriculture.

The city has several shopping areas, from the old traditional souqs to glittering western-style malls. Goods in every sector and price range are

Doha is situated on a wide, sweeping bay *(opposite, top)* which culminates at the northern end in the dramatic landmark building of the Sheraton Hotel *(above and below)*, inspired by the Mesopotamian ziggurat.

available from around the world – everything from local handicrafts and ethnic knick-knacks to designer clothes and the most sought after names in watches and jewellery. Unpaved, narrow twisting alleys have largely been replaced by marble and glass, airconditioning, fountains and indoor plants. Yet some more traditional areas remain, notably in Souq Waqif, the now partly modernised 'Standing Souq'. There you can find the perfume shops which sell essential oils and essences and will mix perfumes to order as well as selling scent from the world's most exclusive perfumiers. It is also in Souq Waqif that you find heaps of myrrh (from the Arabic *murr* meaning bitter), frankincense from Oman (known locally as *luban*), the sweet-smelling essence-rich wood, *oud*, from south Asia and the brown fibrous balls of *bokhur* – mixtures of gums, resins and spices which are burnt over hot charcoal in every Qatari home and passed round as a sign of hospitality after the meal and coffee, alongside a tray of perfumes. The smoke is also used to perfume the fresh laundry. As the *medkhan* (incense burner) is passed around, the men and women (in their separate groups) they will waft the smoke into the clothing. The alleys of Souq Waqif are also the place to find fresh spices of every type and hue, traditional national dress,

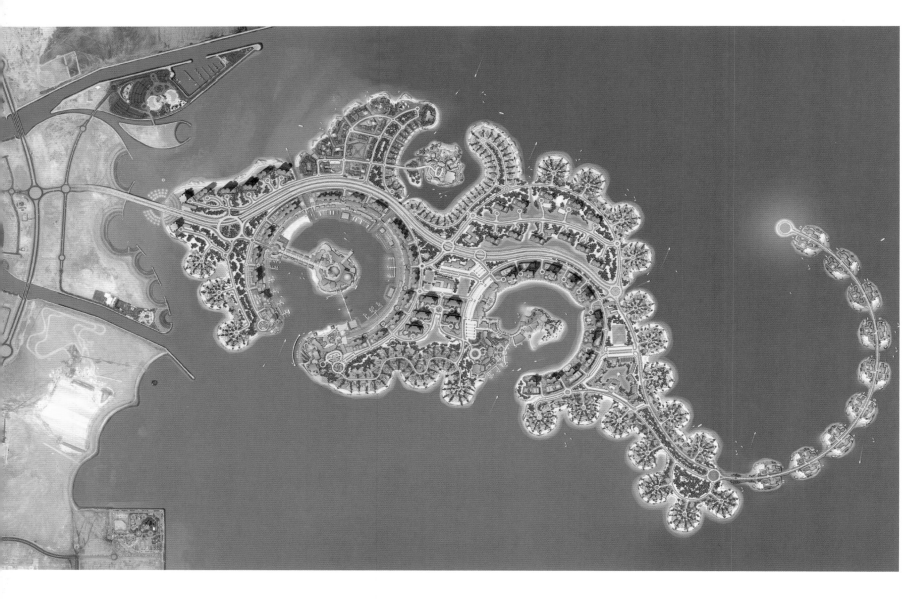

*Realising the Reclamation Opportunity*
The Pearl, a massive land reclamation project creating a
man-made island *(plan above),* reaches out into the waters
of the Gulf, just north of the main bay of Doha *(right),*
which is itself a sculptured coastline created in the 1980s.
The vision of the Pearl project is to create a community
celebrating the best of Arabian and Mediterranean lifestyles
*(right),* with some 7,500 homes designed to accommodate
30,000 inhabitants.

Doha abounds with elegant shopping malls, offering fine goods from all over the world. These modern shopping malls vie with, but do not as yet supplant, the traditional souqs of the region.

Qataris are natural traders (*right*) and will generally drive a hard bargain (*left*).

household items including the huge cooking pots and serving trays, and enormous round dishes of jelly-like sweets, similar to Turkish Delight, cut out and sold by the kilo.

A characteristic of the souqs – both old and modern – is the grouping of vendors by commodity. This is most striking in the gold souqs, where glittering traditional bridal jewellery and modern gemstone pieces can be seen heaped side by side. Window and counter displays, together with open doors point to the absence of theft.

The fish, meat and vegetable markets moved out of the town centre in the 1980s to a new Central Market location between the city centre and the industrial area, where there are also animal, animal feed and falconry markets. New, but traditional, 'weekend' markets have sprung up nearby selling inexpensive imported and locally produced household goods and clothes.

Two huge new malls opened in the year 2000, combining department stores, boutiques and supermarkets with cinemas, restaurants and entertainment facilities. The extensive City Centre mall, overlooking the Corniche, houses the country's first ice-skating rink.

## Around the Coasts

Twelve kilometres south of the capital, Al Wakra is an old fishing and pearling port which until the early part of the 20th century was administratively independent from Doha. Until the 1980s, the road south from Doha International Airport to Al Wakra fishing harbour passed through undeveloped land, and Wakra itself had changed little from its early days. Now it is developing as a thriving satellite of the Doha conurbation. Several of its old mosques have been partially or completely restored, and extensive restoration work has been carried out on one of the old waterfront houses as well as a large fortified house near the harbour. The old fort near the large Friday Mosque shows many features of traditional architecture, but restoration work has not yet begun. A regional museum was opened in a restored building on the waterfront.

Wakra retains the old dhow harbour, but the natural tidal lagoon nearby has been developed with the planting of additional mangrove saplings. The beach has been filled and graded, and sunshades have been erected, with a children's play area in the small park backing onto the beach and cafeteria. There are several pristine beaches both to the north and south of the town, and it is possible to drive right down the coast from Doha to Wakra in a four-wheel drive, deviating only to bypass the power and desalination plant at Ras Abu Fontas.

Further along the coast southwards there rises one of Qatar's designated 'Industrial Cities': Messaieed – formerly Umm Said. The city's administration of the commercial, residential

Boats have held a pivotal role in Qatari life since ancient times (*above*). Traditional fishing and trading craft tell of the commercial roots of the city whose bold modern lines today plank the shoreline of the ancient harbour. The fish markets of Doha (*opposite, below*) feed half the nation.

and industrial areas has passed in its entirety to the State-owned Qatar Petroleum's Messaieed Industrial City Management. These responsibilities include health care.

Development of the 40 sq.km. industrial area and port began in the 1960s, but expansion has been spectacular since the 1990s, with a new clinic and hospital under construction, new housing being developed, a commercial complex and additional leisure facilities and the whole area landscaped with a

'green zone' separating the residential and industrial zones. At an appropriate 15 km. northwest is sited Qatar's new hazardous waste treatment plant.

Messaieed borders an area of spectacular natural beauty, Khor Al Udaid, the Inland Sea, surrounded by crescent-shaped *barchan* sand dunes. Sealine Beach Resort, one of the properties of Qatar National Hotels, lies between Messaieed and Khor Al Udaid on a favoured stretch of coastline. Artificial reefs have

Mending the nets (*above*) and fish traps remains an essential skill.

Skippers and owners take their ease, their savings secure in the bank beyond.

been created offshore for scuba divers investigating the wealth of marine life.

The various industries in Messaieed have developed recreation clubs for their employees and families. The nearby Messaieed Golf Club, with its oil-on-sand course was one of the first in the country.

Forty kilometres north of Doha lies another former pearling port, Al Khor (the name meaning harbour in Arabic). Its landscaped Corniche has shaded beach and picnic facilities, and a protected bathing area for children. An old fortified house on the shore has been converted into a regional museum. The dhow harbour remains an active fishing port with its own Customs Post.

At the turn of the millennium, Al Khor's population was approaching 20,000. A new housing community between it and the village of Al Thakira, serving the northern industrial city of Ras Laffan, heart of the country's natural gas industry, was being created by Qatargas and RasGas, with a population expected to have topped five thousand by 2002.

The harbour at Al Ruwais, at the northern tip of the peninsula, is the centre of an active fishing community. Dhows are moored in the harbour, which has its own Customs Post, and particularly on Friday afternoons the fisherman can be seen making and mending the nets and traps. Several of the old village buildings and mosques are doing good service along the shore. The nearby Medinat Shamal (town of the north) has become an administrative centre for the region, and a new government regional hospital was planned for the early 2000s.

On the western coast of Qatar stands Dukhan, centre of Qatar's onshore oil industry, and the location of the first oil finds in the country. Designated as an Industrial City, it is also managed by Qatar Petroleum (QP). The majority of its residents in the area have some connection with the oil industry. The centre of the community is formed by QP housing, workshops, and wellhead installations. Environmental concerns are a main priority. The town's name (which means smoke) dates back to the days of the early flare-offs from the wells. The community has a golf club as well as a beach and sailing club. The nearby Bir Zikrit peninsula is popular with weekend campers, and day trippers enjoy the unspoilt beaches and shallow waters as well as the spectacularly eroded limestone formations nearby.

Almost in the centre of the Qatari peninsula, Al Shahaniyah is the home of camel racing in the country with an oval race track and grandstand replacing the original straight track further to the

Seaside villages of local stone and clay *(above)* tell of a disappearing style of living and habitation, while many of their inland oasis counterparts *(below and opposite)*, superseded by modern dwellings, are now folk-memory.

race meetings are held every Wednesday from October to May for thoroughbreds, locally bred pure Arabs, and internationally bred pure Arabs. An international Arabian Horse Show is also hosted by the club each year, drawing many of Qatar's social elite.

The purebred Arabian (the 'Arab', or *Aseel*) has been valued throughout history for its courage, endurance and swiftness of foot. The horses are smaller than the racing thoroughbreds in the west, but superior in stamina, and their beauty unparallelled. Nowadays, a number of stud farms in the country are once again breeding these fine horses in the region.

The Aseel was valued by the bedouin as a trusty steed in battle, as swift transport for messengers, and as a symbol of wealth and prestige. Its surefootedness at night in the desert and ability to survive the harsh desert climate are undisputed. In oral tradition, the horse with the white forehead was blessed, the bay was the most enduring and the chestnut was the fastest. When a foal was born, the bedouin would grab the tail, jerking it firmly upwards in the belief it would give it a better 'set'.

In modern-day Qatar, the population may live a life of relative luxury in a country with a high per capita income. But weekend pursuits often reflect the lifestyles of forefathers, with men opting to camp in the desert in the cooler months, or take to the sea for a fishing trip.

**Social Life and Etiquette**

Qatar has steadfastly retained its observance of religious proscriptions and prescriptions, its traditions and its culture, despite its modernisation and contacts with the major western powers. Apart from the requirements of the working environment, Qatari women will socialise with women, and men with men. Although more and more young couples will dine out with their children and friends, it is still traditional for the women to entertain their female friends at home, whilst the men gather nightly in the separate *majlis* or reception rooms of their houses to talk and exchange stories over tea and coffee. Qatari women are taking a more active role in the workforce, but many still prefer to take advantage of 'Ladies Only' timings in shops, recreation clubs, at exhibitions and concerts.

Courtesy is strictly observed. Anyone entering a house, an office, even an elevator or a doctor's waiting room will greet those already there with the phrase *As-Salaam Aleykum*, (Peace Be Upon You), and will receive the reply

south east. Camel breeders and trainers have set up their camps in the desert nearby, and the racetrack attracts thousands of camels, owners, breeders and enthusiasts for two major Gulf tournaments each year. This event is illustrated in Chapter 8. Close to the race track is an oryx park, administered by the Ministry of Municipal Affairs and Agriculture (*see* Chapter 1). Tour companies arrange visits to the park, which also attracts State and private visitors and school parties. Several nearby stud farms breed pure Arab horses.

Hunting was part of the way of life. Gradually, it has developed into sport. The Holy Quran counsels that animals should not be kept as pets, but permits their use as providers of meat milk and fibres, as working animals – camels and donkeys were used as pack animals and for transport, together with the Arab horses of the region – or as aids to hunting. (Animals should be freshly killed for food, meat should never be taken from a previously dead carcass except in life-or-death situations.) The bedouin used dogs, such as salukis to hunt larger game, whilst falconry continues to occupy the leisure time of young and old men alike (*see* Chapter 4).

Camel racing retains its popularity amongst the local population, as does horse racing. The Race and Equestrian Club is based in Al Rayyan, where there is a grass racetrack; weekly

*Aleykum As Salam.* Guests will always be welcomed in the home with tea, coffee, soft drinks and tempting cakes or sweets. Extra food is always prepared at mealtimes, so that unexpected guests can be looked after. Courtesy visits are commonly paid in cases of celebration or bereavement as well as on feast days.

While a number of Qatari families now choose to furnish at least a part of their home in a 'western' style, most will retain at least one traditional room with embroidered or woven floor cushions. In general, regardless of the style of the family rooms, the main reception rooms will have the chairs placed against the walls, so that no guest inadvertently shows discourtesy by turning his back on another.

Once early childhood is over, boys and girls are educated in single-sex state schools, and will socialise separately. Whilst no young person may be married against their will, it is still customary for the marriage to be arranged by the families. Yet it is increasingly common for the young people themselves to participate in the discussions and deliberations. Families are large; preference is generally given to marriages within the extended family. Those wanting to marry an outsider are often reminded that '*Halaawat al thobe roq'ito minoh*', 'a patched *thobe* is more beautiful when the patch is of the same material'. Traditionally, the mother or another female relative of the young man will go to the house of the prospective bride to arrange the match, but only after a canvass of several families with potentially suitable daughters, and consultations with the groom-to-be. Once the alliance has been agreed, the couple can meet in the presence of chaperones ... a different situation to the old bedouin weddings in which the young bride was wrapped up in a carpet to be carried off to the home of her bridegroom, a man on whom she had never set eyes before. There were occasions when the first she knew of her impending marriage was the delivery of the bridal trunk, *al dazzah*.

Although a number of families will pay, or expect to receive, a dowry (which is paid by the groom to the bride, not to her family) the custom is no longer rigidly adhered to. The Government has attempted to discourage large dowries by introducing sponsored 'Mass Weddings' to benefit those with limited financial resources.

The marriage ceremony itself is the legal signing of a contract between the two parties; what is commonly referred to as 'the wedding', to which hundreds of guests will be invited, is the equivalent of a western wedding reception and

may be held weeks later. Only after that will the couple be considered married and take up residence together.

Separate celebrations are held for the bride and groom, the culmination of several days of activity, the groom being escorted to the women's reception to meet and sit with his bride in front of her guests on the final wedding night. The spring months and early summer as well as the cooler months at the end of the year are popular times for weddings, because despite the trend to hold receptions in the five-star hotels, many families will gather out of doors. Tents are likely to be set up for the women, allowing them privacy even when erected on the street; the men will often have huge areas of open ground carpeted, with armchairs set out for hundreds around the perimeter, the whole area strung with lights. The most obvious signs of a forthcoming wedding are the strings of lights hired to bedeck the future bride's home.

'Henna night' is still part of the wedding ritual for a Qatari bride. The decorative paste is applied in intricate patterns to her hands, arms, feet and ankles and to those of her sisters and close friends. Although this originally took place during a ladies-only party in the bride's home and the henna artists were often relations, now many of the girls will visit a beauty parlour instead, or have the beautician visit their house. Qatari brides used to wear the intricately embroidered *Thobe Al Nashl* *(illustrated on page 73)* for their weddings – as for any special occasion – now white designer dresses are increasing in popularity, either imported or made to measure by one of the thousands of skilled tailors and embroiderers in town who produce beading and decorative work which would be the pride of many an *haute couture* house.

Qatari society has always been based on trading. For centuries coastal settlements had harvested pearls and the bedouin had traded livestock and handicrafts. Both types of activity required men to travel, and women played a key role in sustaining the social and economic needs of their community.

The advent of the oil industry has inevitably meant a major transformation of Qatari society within a few decades to a modern welfare state. The role of women in the new society was at first not easy, as the nomadic population settled in urban centres and many of their skills became obsolete. In the new market economy, women were often excluded from the social networks essential for business development, and it became difficult for them to defend their function in a

rapidly changing society. However, education has played a major role. Currently, women students at Qatar University outnumber the men by three to one.

Women's participation in the economy has increased dramatically. In 1970 the percentage of women in the workforce was 2.6; by the end of the century this had risen to 25 per cent, the third highest in the region. In the democratically organised municipal elections of March 1999, women participated freely not only as voters but as candidates for seats. HH the Emir is committed to ensuring gender-equality in terms of rights, responsibilities and opportunities for women, while abiding within the framework of a strictly Islamic society.

Despite her wealth, Qatar has developed differently from other Gulf states. Her people are generally considered, both by other Gulf nationals and by westerners, to be more reserved and modest than their neighbours. Ostentatious display of wealth is frowned upon. Oil or gas booms notwithstanding, Qatar has not indulged in the extravagant, flamboyantly decorated buildings and luxury amenities which characterise other Gulf states. It has preferred a calmer pace.

The result in Doha is a well-planned city where most of the population live in comfortable villas instead of high-rise flats, traffic problems are minimal compared with those of neighbouring states, and the port is kept to a manageable size so that the population can enjoy what is undoubtedly the most beautiful waterfront in the region. Doha Airport can, perhaps, be taken as a representative image of the country: conveniently close to town, it is unpretentious, uncluttered and highly efficient – with none of the swank of the endless walkways, the insistence on duty-free shopping, that typify other Gulf airports.

Yet at festival time – at *Eid*, anniversaries, and National Day (September 3) – the people loosen up in cheerful displays of communal enjoyment. The bag-pipe band of the police will swing through the streets, or a military brass band. A brilliant pageant will delight a packed national stadium.

Or there will be a performance of the traditional *ardha* by men of the desert tradition, with swords and sticks, and drumming and piping. The *ardha* is one of the most popular and enduring dances – and the one performed most frequently at weddings and celebrations. A so-called 'strong' dance which is a display of unity and strength, the *Ardha* can be seen regularly during *Eid* holidays, on National Day

Modern villas (*as above*) provide comfortable family homes. In Doha (*above*), as elsewhere in Qatar, new efficient housing is often gathered in large compounds.

Telecommunications have boomed in Qatar as elsewhere and communication today is easier than it has ever been (*below and opposite*).

A gentle jest in the form of a television aerial links age-old custom with modern life on the roof of the villa (*right*). Balconies grace the neighbours (*below*).

A Scottish influence – in the form of the bagpipe – crept into the cheerful ceremonial face of Doha's musically-inclined police, while the brass brand (*opposite*) makes for admirable public relations for the forces of the law . . . and brings in the recruits.

– which falls on September 3 – and occasions such as the anniversary of the Emir's succession. In pure form, it combines both dance and poetry, with a single poet moving back and forth between two facing lines of singers and dancers, giving each in turn a line to repeat. The men wield intricately decorated swords as the lines move together and apart, lifting them skywards as they repeat the lyrics of horsemanship, chivalry and courage.

Naturally enough, traditional music in Qatar falls into two categories – songs connected with the sea and those reflecting desert life. This musical heritage is discussed more fully in Chapter 4.

Percussion either clapping or drums – plays an important part. The traditional drum is the *tabl*, an oval drum with skins at either end, suspended from a strap around the player's neck, and beaten with a short stout stick. Today's performances of the old songs often also include the *tar*, a large tambourine-style instrument not originally taken to sea. The *tar*'s voice or note is usually adjusted by warming it in front of a camp fire. It is an instrument more commonly seen at weddings and other celebrations.

Finally, there is a small double skinned drum, not much longer than a man's hand, called a *murwas*, which requires much dexterity. to play well.

The drum (*tar*) provides the essential communal beat (*right*).

The *ardha* is a traditional dance that symbolises strength, and martial vigour. *(below)*

# 3 History

Most authorities now agree that there is, at present, no conclusive evidence of Paleolithic man having inhabited the peninsula of Qatar. When the Arabian Gulf was dry, some 70,000 to 44,000 years ago, early man may have wandered what was then a marshy plain, but no signs of human occupation from this period survive.

This late date for the occupation of the whole of eastern Arabia, including Qatar, has only recently been accepted. The pioneering Danish archaeologists who were the first to work in Qatar in the 1950s and 1960s saw no reason to dispute the assumption by their predecessors in the Middle East that the Arabian peninsula had been inhabited for some 55,000 years. The Danish prehistorian Holger Kapel classified a large collection of stone tools into four groups, and in 1967 he published the *Atlas of the Stone-Age Cultures of Qatar*. 'A Group', which he considered the earliest, included massive, primitive-looking hand-axes found on ancient shore-lines far removed from today's coast. The three other principal Stone Age industries which followed culminated in 'D Group', containing superbly-crafted tanged arrowheads.

It was not until the excavations in Qatar by the French mission from 1976 onwards that an entirely new set of dates was assigned to Qatar's pre-history. Excavations at Al Khor on the east coast proved that 'A Group' was not a Paleolithic industry. The site under investigation contained hearths, tools, shells and fish teeth and yielded carbon 14 dates of 5340-5080 and 5610-5285 BC. Nearby was an area covered in flint tools and flakes, representing three clearly-defined levels of occupation. 'A Group' and 'C Group' tools in the same layer, together with a fragment of Ubaid pottery from Mesopotamia, showed that the 'A Group' tool-making industry could not have been either Paleolithic or earlier than the other groups.

The increase in rainfall which occurred between 8,000 and 4,000 BC made eastern Arabia a more hospitable place than it had been previously. It is this period which saw the gradual emergence of Neolithic cultures throughout the Middle East. Domestication of animals and cultivation of plants evolved in Egypt, Turkey, Iraq and Iran. In Qatar, the

wandering population of hunters and gatherers learned to harvest wild cereals. Two limestone querns found at Al-Da'asa on the coast south of Duhkan may have been used for the preparation of wild grains.

The making of pottery is thought to have begun around 6,000 BC. Pottery from Al Ubaid,

Neolithic man living in the region of Al Khor some seven thousand years ago left evidence of his skills in tool making with the scraper illustrated here.

a small site near the ancient city of Ur in Iraq, begins to turn up in Qatar less than a thousand years later. Early Ubaid pottery is thin, greenish in colour, and characterised by lively painted designs in red or dark brown. Since the discovery of Ubaid pottery in the Eastern Province of Saudi Arabia in 1968, it has been found on over 40 sites in Saudi Arabia, five in Qatar and recently at Umm al-Quwain and Ras al-Khaimah in the northern Emirates. Clearly, people were able to travel long distances at that time, making short, coastal hops between

settlements. The earliest craft were probably constructed of bundles of reeds lashed together, or of palm-frond ribs. Small inshore fishing craft made of palm-frond ribs, known as *shashahs*, were in use in the Gulf until a few years ago.

Between about 5,000 and 3,500 BC the coastal areas of Qatar and neighbouring lands

Excavations of Qatar's oldest known fort, at Murwab, yielded a fine example of contemporary work in this vase.

were inhabited by a population which survived by hunting, gathering and fishing, living in temporary campsites to which they returned annually. Middens of shell and fish-bone accumulated at such seasonal sites. No trace of their shelters remain, but possibly they constructed palm-frond huts similar to the barasti which were widespread in the Gulf region until the oil era. Southern Mesopotamian fishermen working the rich fishing banks off the Arabian coast may have visited these sites from time to time to salt and

# ROCK ART

Qatar has a number of rock-carving sites which, with one exception, all occur on limestone jebel outcrops along the eastern and far north-western coasts. The exception is Jarr Umm Tuwaim, some seven kilometres inland from the Bay of Salwa in the south-west, where a single large rock is covered with cupmarks, either single, paired or in double rows, and also *wasm*: camel-brand marks used by the bedouin pastoralists.

The eight major carving sites on Qatar's coast, and Jarr Umm Tuwaim, have certain features in common. Cupmarks arranged in various combinations occur on all the sites, as do shallow, oval or circular flat-bottomed basins, and vertical shafts of up to 0.5 metre in depth. Some of these carvings, especially those at Al Furaihah north of Zubara, are characterised by a number of carved footprints.

Danish archaeologists first noticed the carvings at Jebel al Jusasiyah in 1961, and photographed them the following year, recommending their preservation to the government. In 1974 Hans Kapel studied and recorded the carvings, numbering some 580 sites and making detailed drawings.

Both Kapel and Professor Hawkins, who made a study of the carvings at Jebel al Furaihah in the 1980s, consider that the double rows of cup-marks were used for a game known to archaeologists as 'mancala', a game still played in West Africa and possibly the oldest game in the world. Several 'boards' are carved into the stone surfaces of Khurna temple at Thebes, which dates to 1400 BC. It was played all over the Gulf from Kuwait to Oman, and in Iran, but Qatar, where it was known as Al Haloosah or Al Huwailah, is unique in the sheer number of carvings it depicts. The game is played by two people, who distribute counters into the cups, and the most usual variation is a double row each of seven holes, often with a larger oval hole at the end to hold the counters.

At Al Jusasiyah, Kapel recorded a total of 333 game boards, of which 193 had two rows of seven holes. There are also 71 'rosettes' at Al Jusasiyah and 62 at Al Furaihah, usually with nine holes around a central one. This game was known locally as Al Ailah and as Umm al Judairah in Kuwait and Bahrain.

If the cup marks are indeed game boards, however, the sheer number of them and the wide range of variations in the number of cups, is remarkable. Some are carved on steep slopes where the cups could not have retained the counters, others have holes too small to hold anything larger than a few rice grains. They remain, at present, something of a mystery.

Examples of the series of pitted holes thought to be gameboards (first and third above) and of the different depictions of boats, plan (first and last above) and elevation (second).

The boat carvings at Jebel al Jusasiyah are of great interest, particularly as some depict vessels no longer in use today. They fall into two distinct types: bas-relief designs where the boat is shown in plan, and ships drawn in elevation which have been 'hammered' into the rock with pricked lines, almost certainly done with a metal tool. The 124 bas-relief designs are unique. Fish-shaped, with sharply pointed ends, many have thwarts and the stepping for the mast clearly shown. Some trail anchors, either the metal two-pronged anchor (*bawara*) or the traditional Arab stone anchor (*sinn*) which is a large triangular or round stone with a central hole through which a wooden beam was fixed. The big, two-pronged iron anchor was introduced into the Gulf by the Portuguese in the early 16th century, but smaller 4-pronged grapnels are known to have been in use some 200 years earlier. All of this suggests that the boats with metal anchors cannot be older than 700 years. In some boats a steering oar can be clearly seen. This was the simplest kind of steering and was in general use until the 10th century when Arab mariners invented the rope-operated rudder. Later the Portuguese introduced the tiller, which replaced the rudder and rope system on some craft. Although some of the carved boats appear to have a rudder, steering oars appear to have long survived the introduction of the rudder into the Gulf, and small fishing badans using two steering oars were drawn by a European observer off Muscat in the early 19th century. Many of the boats have oars, depicted at right angles to the boat. There are between 6 and 14 pairs of oars to each boat, although some appear to have a rather haphazard arrangement, with more oars on one side than on the other.

The oared boats depicted here were most probably used for pearling. There is a concentration of pearl banks off the north-east of Qatar and, while anchored on the banks, the boats' oars were left unshipped as supports for the divers. Al Jusasiyah, today almost deserted, could well have played an important role in the pearling industry of the 17th and 18th centuries. It may have been a place where merchants congregated to await the return of the fleet. The quantity of potsherds scattered around the *jebel* largely dates from that period, although a few are earlier.

The seventeen boats drawn in elevation are cruder and rather less elegant than the bas-relief carvings, but in fact they are technical drawings intended to record specific information. One is instantly identifiable as a *bateel* by the high stern and bulbous 'dog's head' projection at the bow. It carries a large triangular sail. The vertical and horizontal division of the hull of this and other boats may be intended to indicate their loading capacity. Another drawing shows a *baqqarah*, once a common coastal craft, but no longer in use today. These boats, with their high sterns and stitched construction, represent a tradition of boat-building pre-dating European influence. Other vessels have been identified as *shu'ai*: smaller boats, still to be seen today, which were used mainly for fishing but also for pearling.

dry their catch, bringing pottery with them and giving it to the local inhabitants or perhaps exchanging it for fresh meat.

The first Ubaid potsherds in Qatar were found by the Danish expedition at Al Da'asa in 1961 but not identified until later. Post-holes from shelters survived at the site, and a poignant find was a neat stack of domestic implements: querns, a grinder, a pounder, a slab of coral.

Whoever piled them so carefully clearly intended to return, but never did so.

Ubaid pottery of a slightly later date than at Al Da'asa was found at Ras Abaruk by the British Expedition of 1973-4. An area 200 metres square yielded not only potsherds but quantities of flint debris and tools amounting to an estimated 11,000 kilos. The amount, plus the bones of mammals, birds and fish, suggests

that the site was of a hunting-gathering-fishing camp visited seasonally over many years.

French excavations on low hills at Al Khor in 1977-8 revealed more pottery from this period, as well as fragments of stone vessels. Between 1977 and 1981, eight cairn burials out of a group of eighteen were excavated, dating from the Ubaid period. Each consisted of an oval pit over which a low cairn of limestone

---

## QATAR ARCHAEOLOGY PROJECT 2000: The World's First Digital Excavation

Four thousand years ago the Arabian Gulf was a centre for international trade. Ivory, precious woods, exotic animals and furs were shipped from the Indian sub-continent up through the Gulf to the cities of southern Iraq. Copper and other valuable metals from what is now the UAE and Oman were shipped up the coast to Bahrain and from there to Iraq.

In January 2000 a team of twelve British archaeologists arrived to spend three months in Qatar at the invitation of the National Council for Culture, Arts and Heritage. They were joined by archaeologists from the Department of Museums and Antiquities. Their objective was to carry out a detailed survey and excavations on a small island in Khor Shaqiq bay on the east coast, to gain more information about the role the island had played in the maritime commerce of the Gulf from the earliest times up to and including the Islamic period. Funding for the project came from the National Council and from the private business sector.

The island, which measures only 600 by 400 metres, is surrounded by a mangrove forest, which provided early inhabitants with wood for temporary shelters and for fuel. A regular food supply was guaranteed by the fish, shellfish and birds which sheltered there.

The project team began by mapping the entire island, with the help of Qatar's internationally renowned GIS (*Geographic Information Systems*) Centre. Satellite-mapping

systems were used to produce a three-dimensional map of the island showing all the geographical features and the archaeological sites. A magnetometer was used to look for buried structures. Some human activities, such as cooking, leave a magnetic 'fingerprint' in the soil that shows up as a high reading when the survey instruments sweep over.

An area on the shoreline was stripped to a depth of 5 cms to ensure any modern contamination was removed. As soon as any object appeared a Global Positioning System

recorded its location, drawings and photographs were digitally produced and descriptions written on electronic notepads trained to recognise individual handwriting. Survey information was recorded on sunscreens 'read' by laptop computers carried in backpacks, and later transferred into a main database, which was also used to create maps, graphs and tables.

During the excavation quantities of red 'Barbar' pottery were found, manufactured in Bahrain c.1950 BC. A fragment from a decorated copper bowl indicated the wealth of the island people of the time. On the same site, some 3,000 years later, large, shallow, stone-lined pits were constructed. Fragments of oyster shell suggest that they were used in a process for retrieving pearls.

This pioneering project has concentrated the attention of archaeologists all over the world on Qatar, as it is the first time that such advanced technology has been employed on an archaeological excavation. Regularly updated information is obtainable on the website www.bufau.bham.ac.uk/qatar/index.htm

Map: Computer model of Al Khor island with location of archaeological features shown as coloured spots. Top left: Blue and white ware. Late Islamic (17th – 18th century AD)

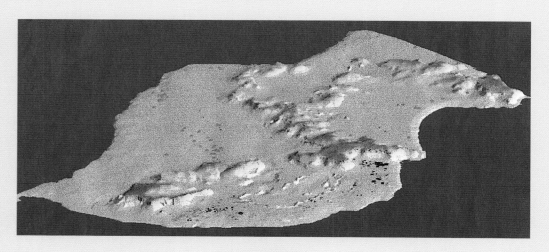

slabs had been erected. Four skeletons in flexed position remained intact. The graves contained shells, and bone and stone beads, including seven of obsidian.

Contact between the people of southern Mesopotamia and those of the eastern Arabian coast, including Qatar, continued over centuries. During the middle of the 4th millenium the world's first walled towns were built in the fertile plain surrounding the Tigris and Euphrates rivers. By the end of the 3rd millenium Sumerian scribes began to make written records: pressing the triangular ends of reeds into clay tablets to make cuneiform letters. Around the same time lived Menes, the Egyptian ruler who united Upper and Lower Egypt and so opened the way for the great civilisation that was to flourish for many centuries along the banks of the Nile. The link between Sumer and Egypt was almost certainly via the Gulf.

In the early 3rd millennium Sumerians settled on Tarut Island, off the Saudi coast some 100 kilometres north-west of Qatar. The earliest inscriptions mentioning 'the land of Dilmun' are understood to refer to the eastern coast including Tarut. Later, from 2450-1700 BC, Dilmun, a peaceful trading civilisation, was centred in Bahrain. Sumerian city states traded silver, textiles, oil and precious resins for building timber, stone and copper. The trade was channelled through the Gulf, and Bronze Age cultures sprang up and flourished along both coasts. Third millennium cuneiform tablets refer to Magan, centred in what is now Oman, and Meluhha in the Indo-Pakistan region.

That Qatar played its part in this complex trading network is evident from the presence of Barbar pottery, a product of the Dilmun civilisation, at two sites: a depression on Ras Abaruk peninsula, and a small island in the bay of Khor Shaqiq, near Al Dakhirah, where excavations by the Qatar Archaeology Project took place in 2000.

By about 1750 BC the local societies of the Gulf had entered a period of apparent decline. Southern Mesopotamia, which had previously acquired most of its foreign materials from the east and south-east, was now reoriented towards the north and west. Kassites from the Zagros mountains had assumed power in the middle of the 2nd millenium, and Dilmun became absorbed into Kassite Babylonia.

The only archaeological site in Qatar dating from this period lies on the southern shores of the small island in the bay of Khor Shaqiq. Here, crimson and scarlet dyes were being produced from a species of murex, a marine snail. Elsewhere, the dye is known as 'Tyrian purple' owing to its large-scale production at the great city of Tyre in the Levant, and Khor Island is the first such site to have been discovered in the Gulf. The middens of crushed shells contain the remains of 3,000,000 snails. Quantities of coarse Kassite pottery was found, the remains of large vats used in the dye production. Scarlet and purple-dyed cloth was much in use in Kassite and post-Kassite Babylonia; its use was controlled directly by the ruler and was confined to immediate members of the royal family and to powerful religious figures. Khor Island provides the first evidence that this dye did not come exclusively from the west.

No evidence of Iron Age settlement has yet been found in Qatar, although elsewhere in

The language of the inscription found in this rock at Al Kharrara, in central Qatar, the only one of its kind found in the lower Gulf, is in Safaitic Arabic. The text invokes the pre-Islamic Nabatean god MNT.

eastern Arabia Iron Age villages have been uncovered, whose inhabitants were cultivating dates and cereals. Camels had been domesticated, first as milk animals and some time later as beasts of burden, as early as the 3rd millenium, and it may be that some of the inhabitants of Qatar had by this time become nomadic pastoralists, herding not only camels but also sheep and goats. The climate was now much drier than in the Neolithic period.

Much later the use of the camel as a riding animal developed, and in the 9th century BC camel-riding Arab warriors make their first appearance. They were the descendants of the Amorites, a people known to the Sumerians and the Hebrews.

By the 6th century BC nomads and settlers were becoming interdependent, not only for the exchange of commodities but for the operation of overland trade, using camels, which was augmenting the traditional trade routes.

Alexander the Great conquered Persia in 326 BC, and then went on to enter the Indian sub-continent, having a substantial fleet constructed near present-day Karachi. He then ordered his Cretan admiral Nearchos to explore the coast of Arabia, in preparation for a proposed conquest of the region. The exploration took place, probing the entrance of the Gulf at Ras Musandam. But Alexander's sudden death, three days before the campaign was due to begin, ended the plan of conquest.

His vast empire was divided among his generals. The eastern portion was taken by Seleucis Nictator, who set up his capital at Seleucia on the west bank of the Tigris. At this time the city of Gerrha, on the eastern coast of Arabia not far from Qatar, became a major centre for both land and sea trade between Arabia and India. Pottery fragments from this period, known as Seleucid, occur in some quantity at Ras Uwainat Ali on the west coast of Qatar and a nearby cairnfield on Ras

Abaruk, consisting of over 100 burial mounds – the largest such concentration in the country – has been provisionally dated to the Seleucid era.

There is further evidence of human activity in Qatar during the Graeco-Roman period in the form of a fish-processing complex, again at Ras Abaruk. A stone building consisting of two rooms and a third open to the sea is located on an old shore-line on the north-west of the small peninsula. Nearby is a mound of fish-bones, and several hearths. Some large smooth pebbles, possibly used as hammers, originate outside Qatar, suggesting that the site probably represents a temporary station where fishermen from elsewhere landed to dry and preserve their catch.

Around 140 BC, the rise to power of the Parthians, a Persian people, had begun to interrupt Graeco-Roman trade between Europe and India via the Arabian Gulf, and the Red Sea became again the main link between Rome and the East. But in 225 AD the Parthians were overthrown and the second great Persian empire, that of the Sassanid dynasty, was established. They established their capital in Mesopotamia at Ctesiphon and reversed the practices of their predecessors, controlling the trade of both the Gulf and the Indian Ocean and forcing the decline of the Red Sea as a rival commercial route. By 570 AD they succeeded in extending their control as far as the Yemen. Both sea and land trade routes were arteries, not only of trade, but of cultural influence.

The Sassanids traded a vast range of commodities and it is possible that Qatar contributed two luxury items: purple dye and pearls, to Sassanid trade. A number of areas in Qatar provide archaeological evidence of the involvement of local people with the outside world during this period. At Mezruah, north-west of Doha, an oval burial cairn contained two skeletons, one with an arrowhead embedded in a bone of the forearm. A fine iron sword and some iron arrowheads lay in the grave, which also contained an almost intact Sassanian glass. An intriguing feature was the hamstringing of camels around the grave: early literature refers to the sacrifice of camels around the grave of a hero, and also of horses. Near Umm-el-Ma' on the north-west coast a small settlement contained fragments of glassware and pottery including 'Sassanian-Islamic' glazed ware, and a fragment of red, polished ware dating to the 2nd to 3rd centuries AD. Such finds are evidence of a standard of living well beyond subsistence level.

A map of the region of Qatar at the time of the coming of Islam indicates the significance of Qatar as a link between the Sassanid Empire and neighbouring kingdoms of the Arabian Peninsula.

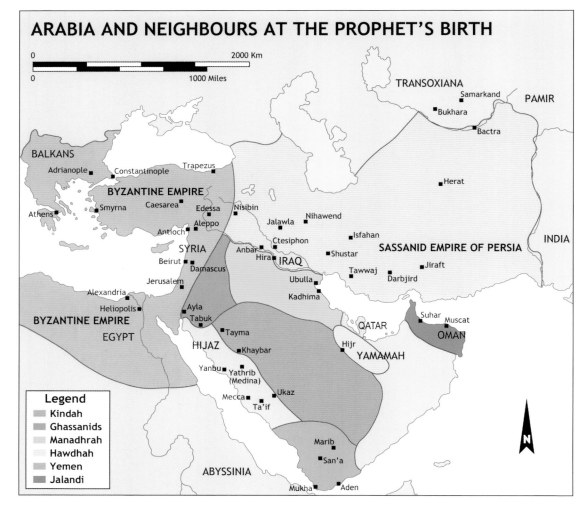

ARABIA AND NEIGHBOURS AT THE PROPHET'S BIRTH

The Zubara fort *(left)* was built in 1938 by Sheikh Abdullah bin Qassim Al-thani as a police outpost and has been used by the military as recently as the 1980s. The ruins of the historic northern city of Murwab nearby remain preserved *(below)*.

## The Coming of Islam

By the end of the 7th century Islam had spread throughout the whole of the Arabian peninsula, ending the paganism practised by much of its population. Politically, the 3rd to 7th centuries AD had seen a reversal in the fortunes of the Arabs of eastern Arabia. The trading opportunities they had once enjoyed had reverted to the control of the Sassanids, Byzantines and others. The call to embrace Islam came in 627-9 AD and the Christian governor of the Hasa Oasis in the Eastern Province of Saudi Arabia quickly adopted the new faith and sent a delegation to the Prophet in Medinah. Others followed suit. Within a short time Islam had helped to do away with the old tribal rivalries by teaching the equality and brotherhood of all Muslims. This new ideology was to provide an inspiration to Arab Muslims and introduce a new era of expansion and exploration, as Islam was taken to the furthest corners of the civilised world.

In 750 AD the Umayyid dynasty, based in Damascus, was overthrown by the Abbasids, who were descended from the uncle of the Prophet. The capital was relocated to Baghdad and this had far-reaching political and economic implications for the Gulf as, inevitably, trade benefited from the wealth and sophistication of the Abbasid empire. This was the golden age of trade in the Gulf, which was to last until the

10th century. Merchants traded with India, China and East Africa and the port of Suhar in Oman rose in importance. This period of adventures by merchant seamen gave rise to the stories of Sindbad the Sailor. The demand in Abbasid Baghdad for pearls undoubtedly enriched the pearl fishers and merchants of Qatar; however, few accounts of Qatar's fortunes exist from this period. The geographer Yaqut al Hamawi, who died in 1229, referred to rough red woollen cloaks being exported from Qatar, and also commented that the markets for horses and camels in Qatar were renowned.

The inland settlement of Murwab near Zubara dates from this period. It consists of some 250 houses, a fort and two mosques. The fort is the oldest in the country and was built on the site of a still earlier fort which was destroyed by fire. The style of both is similar to forts in Iraq dating from the 8th to 9th centuries. Sherds of fine quality ceramics and glassware give a hint of the relative affluence of the town-dwellers. Two other smaller settlements in the area are contemporary. Murwab is the only sizeable ancient settlement in Qatar not situated on the coast.

In the 13th century AD the island of Hormuz, at the mouth of the Gulf, established itself as a new maritime power and by the mid 14th century had gained control of Gulf trade. The Gulf entered into a new period of prosperous commerce and Hormuz became

famous among the European trading nations. In 1498 the Portuguese confirmed a direct sea route to India by rounding the Cape of Good Hope, and they set out to create a new maritime empire. Their aim was to divert the rich trade from India and the Far East to Europe via the Cape, away from the Red Sea and the Gulf. Amid scenes of extraordinary brutality on the part of the conquerors, one by one the Arab ports fell to the Portuguese. In 1515 Hormuz was captured by Admiral Albuquerque and, shortly afterwards, Bahrain. In 1520 Qatif in eastern Saudi Arabia was sacked. Throughout the 16th century, Hormuz remained the base from which the Portuguese controlled the Gulf as far as Bahrain.

Meanwhile, in the northern Gulf, the Ottomans from Turkey had established power, taking over Basra in Iraq between 1534 and 1546 and making several unsuccessful attempts to dislodge the Portuguese from their strongholds. But eventually the task of maintaining control over the Indian Ocean routes, so far from home, proved beyond the resources of the Portuguese. In 1622 the Safavi ruler Shah Abbas I of Persia, allied with Britain, ousted the Portuguese from Hormuz. Fort after

fort fell to the allies, and the Portuguese were finally expelled from Muscat in 1650. They continued to trade in the Gulf, as did the Venetians, but their days of power were over. Between 1630 and 1700 the Dutch East India Company, set up in 1602, dominated Gulf trade, along with the English East India Company which had been formed two years previously. Portuguese trade had been monopolised directly by the crown, but this was a new era of 'merchant adventurers' from Holland, England and later, France.

Ottoman power was gradually weakened. In 1620 the Persians took control of Basra; even so Ottoman authority persisted in a reduced form until 1680, when it yielded to the ascendancy of the indigenous Arabs under the leadership of the Bani Khalid, who dominated eastern Arabia.

As for Qatar itself at this time, life continued to centre around the immemorial activities of pearling and fishing, with bedouin pastoralists grazing the interior. The main east coast settlements were Al Wakrah, Al Bidda' (later to become Doha), Al Huwailah and, in the north Al Ghuwairiyah. Al Huwailah emerged as the principal pearling port of the early 18th century.

On the north-west coast, Murair fort was

What is today's National Museum (*above and above right*) was – from a century and a half ago – Doha's principal and sheikhly fort, now superbly restored. When Doha was established as the principal city, in the early nineteenth century, the cannon (*pictured above left*) was the most feared weapon of war.

Al Khor was, until the 1930s, the centre of the peninsula's vibrant pearling industry, commemorated (*right*) by a traditional *boum* perched overlooking the bay.

built in 1768 to protect Zubara from land attack, and the following year a ship canal two kilometres in length – a remarkable engineering achievement for the period – was dug from the sea to the fort, to facilitate the unloading of supplies. Zubara remained vulnerable from the sea for the next hundred years.

Meanwhile, in 1745 Sheikh Mohammed bin Abd al Wahhab began preaching adherence to orthodox Islam, and this led to a powerful reformist movement which swept the region. It was taken up by the Al Saud of Najd, who reached Al Hasa in 1793, replacing the Bani Khalid. Zubara gave shelter to some of the refugees from Al Hasa, and as a consequence of this Zubara was besieged in 1795 by the Saudi commander, along with Al Huwailah.

By 1820 the British had grown concerned that turbulence in the Gulf could interfere with their trade with India, where they had become the imperial power. Their intervention among the ruling sheikhs resulted in a General Treaty of Peace. The following year Qatar was deemed to have broken the new treaty and the East India Company's cruiser *Vestal* bombarded Doha with their cannon, setting the town on fire – although few of the inhabitants of Doha knew of the treaty's existence. The first Maritime Truce taking effect from 1832, and brokered by the British, helped to outlaw warfare during the pearling season from May to November, and the truce was generally popular. But in 1841 a further bombardment of Doha was launched by the British. A more serious breach, however, was to take place in 1867 when Doha and Wakrah were sacked by a combined force of ships and men from Bahrain and Abu Dhabi. The following June the Qataris, although outnumbered, courageously counter-attacked Bahrain.

*Zubara's fort (top), seen here in an early photograph, has today been restored to a pristine defensive glory.*

*Wakrah's earlier prosperity (now returned to it) is demonstrated by the classical magnificence of various of its fine mercantile houses such as that pictured middle left.*

*Social discourse in the majlis (left) tells of the grace of ancient Qatari custom – shared throughout the Arab world.*

## The Emergence of Al-Thani

The upshot of this conflict was the receipt of compensation by Qatar, and the emergence of Sheikh Mohammed bin Thani Al-Thani as the most influential man in the country. Sheikh Mohammed had recently moved from Fuwairat to Doha. The family stemmed from the Arab tribe Tamim, whose descent is traced back to Mudar Bin Nizar in the eastern parts of the Arabian peninsula.

The treaty ratified on 12 September 1868 effectively marked the end of interference on mainland Qatar by the country's neighbours, and the consolidation of Mohammed bin Thani's status as the internationally recognised ruler of his country

The eclipse of Saudi power in the later 19th century led to renewed interest of the Ottomans in the Arabian peninsula. They sent a deputation to Doha to persuade Qasim, the son of Mohammed bin Thani, to accept the Turkish flag. The British did not intervene, but made it clear they recognised no Turkish rights to Qatar. The following year, 1872, saw the arrival of Turkish troops in Doha and the occupation of a fort. For the next forty years Qasim bin Mohammed Al-Thani charted a course between the Ottomans and the British. Qasim was a man of courage, tenacity and skill, and managed to maintain his position as the chief personage and recognised ruler of Qatar while balancing the two super-powers. But he resented Turkish interference in Qatar's internal affairs and their increasingly oppressive demands for tribute.

Matters came to a head when the Ottoman Wali of Basra, Nafiz Pasha, paid a visit to Qatar in 1893, accompanied by 300 cavalry and a regiment of infantry. Qasim retired to his fort at Wajbah, some 15 kilometres west, and declined the Wali's invitation to visit Doha. On 26 March 1893 Nafiz Pasha made a surprise attack at night on Qasim's headquarters, but the Qatari warriors bravely routed the attackers, who withdrew to Doha Fort.

The Ottoman defeat was a landmark. Qasim's reputation and popularity were firmly established. Although he went into semi-retirement soon afterwards, allowing his brother Ahmad, and later his son Abdullah, to deputise for him on many matters, he continued to exercise control over broad policy. He constructed roads to connect the main towns of the country, and set up religious schools and one secular school. On his death at an advanced age in 1913, Abdullah succeeded him.

In 1915 the last of the Turks left. By this time Britain and Turkey were fighting on opposite sides

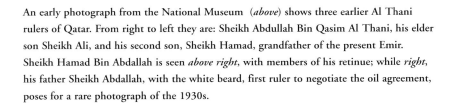

An early photograph from the National Museum (*above*) shows three earlier Al Thani rulers of Qatar. From right to left they are: Sheikh Abdullah Bin Qasim Al Thani, his elder son Sheikh Ali, and his second son, Sheikh Hamad, grandfather of the present Emir. Sheikh Hamad Bin Abdallah is seen *above right*, with members of his retinue; while *right*, his father Sheikh Abdallah, with the white beard, first ruler to negotiate the oil agreement, poses for a rare photograph of the 1930s.

in the First World War. The Anglo-Qatari Treaty of 1916 guaranteed British protection of an independent Qatar from both land and sea attack on the premise of Qatar's neutrality in the World War, and secured the establishment of postal and telegraphic services in Qatar. The World War left prevailing authority in the region with the British. Meanwhile, nationalistic movements were arising in countries bordering the Gulf.

The 1930s saw a time of severe economic hardship when the Western world was in the grip of a recession and the demand for pearls fell. In 1933 the Japanese developed the cultured pearl, dealing a crippling blow to the Gulf pearl industry from which it never recovered. The population of Qatar at this time dropped steeply.

At this low ebb in the fortunes of Qatar, a new hope appeared. Although the possibility of the existence of oil in the region had been realised as early as 1908, when oil was discovered in southern Iraq, followed by a treaty in 1913 with the ruler of Kuwait securing for British companies rights to oil exploration, little happened in the southern Gulf for many years. It was not until the American oil company Socal struck oil in Bahrain in 1932 and then negotiated a concession with Ibn Saud, that the British began to take an active interest in the oil potential of the Arabian peninsula. They focused their attention on Qatar.

News of the attractive terms offered by Socal to Ibn Saud reached Qatar, and the British had to convince Abdullah that he should favour the more modest offer made by the British-controlled Iraq Petroleum Company (IPC). No one was yet to know the true potential of the oil which lay beneath their territory and any geological evidence was largely the preserve of the oil company, which took care not to exaggerate to Abdullah his country's potential. However, he proved a shrewd negotiator, and was able to extract from the British various concessions, including further guarantees from external attack. On 17 May 1935 a document was signed granting the Anglo-Persian Oil Company, a participator in IPC, exclusive rights for production, refining and marketing of petroleum, as well as for natural gases and other by-products. After a series of down payments, Abdullah was to receive royalties of 3 rupees per ton.

Although the presence of petroleum was established in October 1939 (in Dukhan), it was not until 1949 that the first ship left Qatar with the commodity. In an aerial photograph (*above*) taken in the 1960s from above the Al Khuleifat district in the south bay, the former royal palace, now restored as the National Museum, is visible in the centre. The photograph *below*, shows one of the last pearl-fishing teams in operation, in the 1940s – four *ghais* (divers) in the water, each with two ropes, one for hoisting the baskets of oysters from the seabed, and one – on response to a sharp tug from below – to pull up the diver himself. Divers would remain below, at a depth of up to twelve metres, for as long as two minutes, repeatedly – twenty times or more in one hour.

### The Discovery of Oil - and its Consequences

Oil was finally discovered at Dukhan in October 1939, but the Second World War put a stop on production. In 1942 the three appraisal wells were sealed and the company's staff packed their bags: prosperity was to be delayed. Meanwhile, there was more hardship, with the sharp fall in revenue from pearling, and food shortages. Many Qataris temporarily emigrated. It was not until December 1949 that the first ship left the shores of Qatar bearing a consignment of crude oil.

By 1944 Sheikh Abdullah had handed over much of the management of the country's affairs to his son Hamad, a popular leader, respected for his faith, ability and breadth of vision. Yet Hamad himself suffered ill health, and died in 1948, while his young son Khalifa was still being prepared to succeed in his role. Ali, Hamad's eldest brother, was appointed ruler in 1949 when Abdullah abdicated because of old age, with Khalifa bin Hamad as the Heir Apparent. In 1960 Ali abdicated in favour of his son Ahmad, with Khalifa as Deputy Ruler. Then in February 1972 Khalifa assumed power from his cousin, endorsed by the ruling family and the people of Qatar. The country had become formally independent of Britain's protectorate role in the September of the previous year.

In June 1995, Sheikh Hamad bin Khalifa Al Thani acceded to power. His son Sheikh Tamim was appointed Heir Apparent on 5 August, 2003.

Within the two decades following the first production of oil, the country was transformed. The first priority was for education, and in 1956 the state education system was set up and the first generation of boys and girls attended modern schools. The University of Qatar opened in 1973. Hospitals were built from the 1960s, and in 1982 Hamad General Hospital opened in central Doha, one of the foremost hospitals in the Gulf.

The top picture shows how Doha looked on its approach by sea in the later 1960s. To the left, at the same period, is seen the central square, around which all buildings have now been replaced, except for the Clock Tower, then under constructions. *Above*, a Doha policeman at an intersection masters the traffic at the same period.

Characteristic of the old Doha that the coming of oil was to change – and largely sweep away – in the 1950s, were the often exquisitely conceived and executed teak doorways and architraves, such as that pictured *right*. The traditional *Bismillah*, seeking God's blessing on the premises, is carved into the architrave atop the central fluted column.

# 4 The Culture and its Roots

Until the 1920s and 1930s and the decline of Qatar's pearling industry, the population could be roughly divided into two distinct groupings: those dwelling in coastal areas, whose livelihood was closely linked to the sea and the nomadic bedouin tribes which depended for their existence on animal husbandry and trading in products derived from their herds of camels, goats and sheep. For both groups, life was harsh. But they shared certain common factors: strong family ties; community values; the ability to work as a team; perseverence; acceptance; faith in Allah.

Help was willingly given and hospitality was considered to be of the essence. Women were involved in physical work as well as the everyday care of the family; division of labour depended on the extent to which the men's work took them away from the camp or the village, and children worked alongside the adults from an early age.

Education was of the practical rather than academic kind – from the school of life – and oral tradition was strong. Story-tellers and poets filled

the dark evenings around the fires as groups gathered to share their experiences and to join in the ritualistic serving of tea and coffee. Information on family trees, inter-tribal relationships and significant events in history was passed by word of mouth from one generation to the next, and great store was placed in maintaining tradition. The climatic conditions played an important role in the lives of both the desert dwellers and seafarers and both became adept at recognising and predicting changing patterns in the weather. The sailors knew which air and sea conditions favoured particular fishing grounds and also the depth at which the shoals would be found. Almost imperceptible changes in the sky or in the colour of the water would warn them of storms still several hours away. The bedouin, meanwhile, knew almost to the minute for how many days or hours strong winds would last, and their animal husbandry depended on seasonal characteristics. Camels, for example, were bred so that the young were born after the first rains when the desert would be relatively green and the herds would have no problem in

The confident and elegant Islamic lines of Doha's fort now enclose the country's National Museum (*left*).

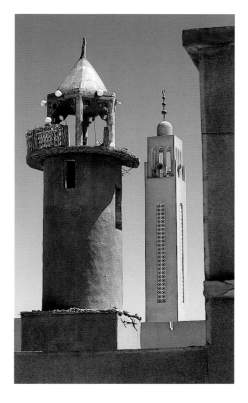

Minarets (*right*) of the northern coastal village of Abu Dhalouf tell of the local architectural inventiveness of successive generations.

Doha remains a centre for trading in the world's store of natural pearls, still treasured by the discerning.

foraging for food; the strongest and healthiest animals, they said, would be the ones born at that time of year.

Song and dance reflected the working environment or celebrated special occasions and festivals. Musical instruments were simple, and percussion played an important part, from simple clapping to the complex rhythms tapped out on clay jars and different forms of drum. Life was dominated by work, the family and the tribe; apart from the few rich merchants, most families lived at subsistence level, growing or catching their own food, making their own garments and creating, repairing and modifying work implements or household artefacts.

The advent of the oil industry brought with it many changes. Many moved away from their traditional occupations, and nomadic lifestyles gave way to permanent settlements. But in the transitional period, bedouin camps acquired tools, implements and materials which were previously alien to their way of life, as did the traders and craftsmen in town. Old tyres and inner tubes were used to make receptacles – or even shoes – where animal hides had been used before. Discarded oilfield equipment was transformed into tripods and lengths of flex or cable replaced the handmade ropes.

## Pearls and Pearling

For thousands of years, natural pearls have been valued for their beauty – and their scarcity, and until the development of Japan's cultured pearl industry, pearling formed the backbone of Qatar's economy. Diving for pearls is no more, although pearl trading survives. At the beginning of the 20th century, there were almost 13,000 men engaged in pearl fishing in Qatar, working from over 800 dhows. However, the industry was on the decline even before the cultured pearl made its first appearance, figures from 1928 showing a substantial decrease in the number of pearling boats fishing off Qatar's shores.

Trading documents from Mesopotamia dating from 2000 BC refer to 'fish eyes' imported from the Gulf, and academics believe it was a reference to the region's superb natural pearls, which have probably been harvested for over 4,000 years. The pearl oyster is a bivalve mollusc found on the sandy bottom, rocky substrate and coral reefs of the shallow waters surrounding Qatar and many of the old oyster beds or *hayr* were in locations now developed as oilfields. Maps do exist of the oyster beds, but crews relied on the knowledge and navigational capabilities of a good captain, who knew both

the location and the depth of each bed.

Though man learnt that pearls were not, in fact, 'fish eyes' it was hundreds of years before he began to understand the way in which they were formed. Fables abounded. Some said pearls were angel's teardrops, others that they were dewdrops fallen to the seabed. Pearls, as we know now, actually consist of minute crystallites of calcium carbonate, arranged both radially and in concentric layers and it is the overlapping platelets of aragonite on the surface which give them their characteristic sheen.

Qatari pearl merchants are still in business. They have a name for each shape, colour and size of pearl.

Most are creamy white. Yet pearls are found in myriad colours – from deep grey to pink or peach. Shapes, too, vary. It could take a merchant 30 years to collect enough pearls, matched in colour and graded in size, to make a perfect necklace. The merchants assessed each single pearl – *igmush* – for colour, shape, size and imperfections. (Common measures for weighing the pearls were the Chao and the Mithgal, with one Mithgal equal to about 4.8 grams. Each Mithgal was divided into 24 Ratti.) The pearls were first graded by means of a series of brass or copper sieves called *tus*. Those

The roots of Qatar's pearling industry lie in thousands of years of history. Diving for pearls from sail-driven craft (*as left*) employed more than half of able-bodied male Qataris a hundred years ago.

retained in the largest sieve were known as *ras* (head, or 'top'); those in the next sieve were *batn*, in the third *thail* or *zayl,* and in the next *ruweiba*. The minute seed pearls passing through even the smallest sieve mesh were known as *alsahtat*. By rolling the pearl under one fingertip, the merchant sought out imperfections; those not perfectly spherical were *barouque*. *Dana* is a large, perfectly shaped pearl, with a good colour and lustre, while *Jiwan* or *Jewana* has a slightly pinkish hue. *Galwa* is perfectly spherical, but has some defects; *Siggine* are tear-drop shaped; *Badlah* is lacking in colour; and *Yakkah* is an imperfect medium sized pearl. A trained eye could also spot the *majhoolah* or 'unrevealed' pearl which contained a perfect pearl within a misshapen exterior and from which a skilled hand could peel off outer layers using a small sharp blade. The most superior black pearl is *Jabassi*, an ordinary black pearl is *Khardil*; *Sofri* is yellow, and *Sindaali* apricot or flesh coloured. Elongated, cylindrical shaped pearls are *Adasi*, the tear-shaped *Sujani* and blister pearls *Nimro*. Pearl merchants tie each type into red muslin bundles.

The smooth inside of the oyster shell is radiant with creamy pastel colours – the nacre

Immemorially, Qatar has been linked to the sea and its craft. *Above*, a shipwright scrapes clean a hull, while *left* a traditional *boum* is preserved in miniature for museum display.

or 'mother of pearl'. If a fragment of grit or any foreign body enters between the mantle and the shell, the oyster secretes additional nacre to envelop it, in effect cementing the irritant to the inside of the shell and forming a lump known as a blister pearl. Freely moving spherical pearls form when the irritant is something like a small worm which cannot be cemented to the shell, and the pearl develops instead within the body of the oyster.

The pearl fishermen would set sail three times a year – a roughly 40 day period beginning in the middle of April, *hansiyah*; for *ghaus al kabir,* a gruelling three and a half months from the end of May to the second week of September, and a final approximately three week period at the end of September and early October, known as *raddah*. Some pearl fishermen spent up to six months at a time at sea, having taken loans from the boat owners to buy provisions in advance to sustain their families. (An initial advance of about 500 Indian Rupees – the currency at the time – was referred to as the *Teskam* or primary contract.)

With the complex division of labour, each ship had: a captain (*nokhda*); pearl divers (*ghasah*); men to pull the divers up from the sea bed, (*siyub*); several additional hands called *radfah* or *radif*, servants called *tabbab* and occasionally apprentices, *walaid*. Small boys, as young as ten, had the task of catching fish to feed the crew, cooking and making the coffee. Over five to ten years, the apprentices would progress from the simpler tasks to the responsible jobs of rope or sail pullers. Each boat also had a lead singer – the *nahham*. Music and dance had an important role on board. Crews were divided into two groups, one singing, clapping and playing percussion instruments like the *gahlah* or *tabl* to spur on their working colleagues. One writer, Toufic Kerbage, refers to the pearling dhows as: 'literally a school of music, because the singing, clapping and beating of rhythms never stops from dawn until sleeping time'.

Depending on the weather and water conditions, the average *ghasah* would make between 10 and 50 dives (*tabbah*) per day, each of up to one and a half minutes, resting briefly in the water between dives. An exceptional diver could make up to ninety dives and remain under water for between two and three minutes. The only true break they took was at the time of mid-day prayers. After praying they would drink coffee – returning to their labour about an hour later. The divers used turtle shell nose clips, called *fatm*, and to protect their fingers from the sharp coral, rough shells and dragon fish they wore finger stalls made of leather called *khabat*. The

The *sambuk* serves as a useful inshore vessel among local fishermen (*right*).

The *qalaleef* - boat builders - of Qatar have long been famed throughout the Gulf for the seaworthiness of their craft - exemplified by the various styles of *boum* illustrated *right* and *opposite*.

Larger Qatari craft such as the high-pooped *bagala* (*above and opposite*) have for centuries sailed the Indian Ocean as merchant vessels.

only other aids they used were wax earplugs.

In order to reach the sea bed swiftly, the divers placed one foot into a looped rope with a lead weight, whilst a second rope, *ida*, was tied around the waist. A tug on the rope would signal to the *saib* on deck that the diver was running out of breath and wanted to return to the surface.

The oysters were collected in a small bag or basket called *dayeen*, which was emptied onto the deck after each dive. The work continued until just before sunset. The main meal of the day would be eaten after sunset prayers, after which the crew would sometimes sing or dance, led once again by the *nahham*. If other pearling boats were working nearby, the crews would sometimes converse with each other, some captains choosing to spend their whole trip in the vicinity of one large oyster bed, others moving to different sites. The crews depended on the captains to locate the most productive *hayr*, situated at depths accessible to his divers, most of whom worked to around 8-10 fathoms. The most skilled could collect oysters from beds up to 14 fathoms.

Small knives with curved blades called *meflaka* were used to pry the shell apart – always under the watchful eye of the captain, who kept all the pearls for the merchants, *tawwash*, during the season. The accounts for all the sales were kept by the ship's accountant, *bendar*. No diver knew if it was the oysters he collected which contained the pearls. Money from the sale of the pearls was divided between the captain and crew according to a strict formula. In a poor season, the men barely earned enough money to cover their loans, but Qatar was well known for having pearl divers who remained free and out of debt and who were generally regarded as among the most successful of the region.

The working day was long; food was dates, rice and fish; fresh water was always in short supply, fresh fruit and vegetables non-existent. Work was exhausting, yield was unpredictable, health hazards were numerous and storms at sea a constant threat. Many divers suffered from respiratory diseases, and the repeated restriction of oxygen to the brain also created many problems. Before the start of the season, many divers would visit traditional medicine practitioners, who would 'bleed' them, taking small quantities of blood from the back of the neck, sucking it out into a glass cone, the incision treated with ash to prevent infection. Another form of treatment which the divers often requested was the application of a hot iron to the external ear canal, possibly to melt ear wax buildup, a common cause of ear-ache.

Teak imported - in Qatari craft - from India and Africa have long provided the planking for locally-built Qatari craft. Wooden dowels have traditionally been preferred to nails in the rivetting of the planks.

diesel-engined dhows. It started life as a much smaller vessel, used occasionally as a diving vessel but more commonly by the pearl merchants. The largest of all was the *baggarah*, with raked stem and tall stern. The *sambuk* had a relatively flat keel for shallow water, and was frequently used for pearl diving as was the light *jalibut*. The swift *bateel*, originally with two masts, is today the term for a large dhow, used for celebratory occasions and as a tourist boat. Another boat with a shallow keel, the *shu'ai*, is used mainly for fishing. The little *houris*, used as a tender for the pearling dhows, figures in many old Qatari proverbs.

## Fishing

Fishing was and is a means of earning a livelihood as well as providing sustenance for the family. Several techniques were employed. Most survive in various forms to the present day; but for editorial convenience the past tense shall be mostly used here.

Simple lines or throw-nets, *saliyeh* were used from the shore. Various tidal traps were built in shallow water at numerous places around the coast the *maskar* – parallel walls of limestone forming such traps – are visible from the shore. At high tide, the fish swim in over the walls to feed inshore; as the water drains at low tide, the fish were trapped and harvested with the aid of a three-pronged spear. *Maskars* along the north coast and in some other areas are still regularly used and maintained. Another inter-tidal trap, *hazra*, comprised cotton gill nets strung between upright poles and forming an entry channel leading to a circular catchment area. Cotton gill nets were also set out parallel to the shore, using date palm logs as floats and stones as sinkers to hold the nets in place. The mesh varied according to the fish sought: two-finger width for medium fish, four-finger for larger *channad* (king mackerel) and tuna. Shrimp nets, also of cotton, were used in shallow water, two or three men wading chest deep, drawing the net ends together to trap the shoals. Shore nets called *yarof* or *degige* are still used, sometimes set out by fisherman in small dhows known as *banosh*. A technique no longer employed is that of narcotising the fish using plant extracts in shrimp paste pellets scattered in the shallows.

To this day fishing boats sail from Doha, Al Khor, Wakrah and Al Ruwais, laden with the domed fishing traps known as *gargoor*. Once traps made from palm ribs, they are now made on the jetties from metal piping and wire mesh

## Boatbuilding

The *qalaleef* – boatbuilders – of Qatar were famed for their skills. In a desert country where timber has to be imported, it is a costly commodity. Traditional ships were built without plans being committed to paper. Axes, adzes, and bow-drills shaped the main beams of teak imported from East Africa and India. The planks were rivetted by wooden dowels or 'sewn' together with twine. Pastes of lime and cattle fat, *shammu*, were used to seal the hulls while

above the waterline oil – from shark or turtle – was applied. The planks were caulked with fibres soaked in sesame seed oil (*simsim*), fish or coconut oil. Prows were painted, usually white, black and pale blue. In the 1930s and '40s lateen sails were replaced or augmented by diesel engines. Qatari boats plied not only the waters of the Gulf, but the Arabian Sea from India to East Africa. The generic term 'dhow' for ocean-going Arab craft is a Swahili word.

The *boum* is today commonest of the larger

Among the men of the coastal population of Qatar, boats have for generations provided a floating home (*above*).

A skipper's most treasured possessions are kept in finely carpentered, often brass studded, chests (*right*).

Locally harvested fish remains the chief source of protein for the coastal population (*far right*).

The aristocratic sport of the bedouin has long been that of falconry. The *saqr - above left -* is trained to precise obedience by its falconer, in pursuit of the traditional prey, McQueen's bustard - the *houbara, left.*

The bedouin way of life has slipped into history - but its skills and crafts remain - as with the camel rider (*below*).

Weaving the traditional 'black tent' of the bedouin was always the task of the women, using yarn from the hair of sheep, goats and camels. The weaver's craft (*right*) using contrasting colours in traditional styles draws on past skills for today's storage bags, rugs and cushion covers.

imported from India. The domes have a conical entrance, narrowing to an aperture through which fish are lured by the bait within, where they find themselves trapped. *Gargoors* are lowered onto the sea overnight.

Fishing is a popular activity as well as a profession. The country's Ministry of Municipal Affairs and Agriculture controls commercial fishing to prevent depletion of the various species.

## Bedouin Hospitality

For the modern Qatari as for the bedouin, emphasis is placed on hospitality. In the desert, and in the coastal villages the serving of coffee had great significance. Business was never discussed before the coffee was served. Coffee was prepared by the men – and often by the youngest adult male. Although the traditional *dallah* (coffee pot) would remain on the fire all day, a new pot would be brewed for honoured guests. The green coffee beans would be taken from the storage container – often a decorated cylindrical box with a conical lid – and roasted over the fire on a roasting pan (*mihamas*) which resembled a huge spoon. The beans were turned using an iron stirrer, sometimes inlaid with brass and

copper. The fire was tended with bellows (*minfakh*), decorated with brass studs and coloured beads. Once the beans were a light golden brown, they were tipped onto a wedge-shaped tray (*mubarad*) to cool, from which they were poured into a brass pestle and mortar for grinding.

Once ground, the beans were placed in the *dallah*, and boiling water poured over them. The coffee maker would open the cardamom pods, crush the seeds in the mortar and add them to the pot, once again bringing the contents to the boil.

With the coffee ready to be served, the coffee maker would pass round a plate of dates, then with the small traditional handle-less cups stacked in his right hand and the coffee pot in his left, pass amongst the guests, first pouring a few drops into a cup and tasting it in front of them. Then, according to age and seniority, he would serve his guests, each time filling the top cup in the stack by about one third. When all the cups in the stack had been handed out, he would return to each of the guests, refilling their cup until, rapidly tilting it from side to side, they returned it to him, indicating they had had enough.

Such coffee rituals persist to this day among Qatari hosts.

## The Bedouin

The seasonal migrations of Qatar's main nomadic tribes traditionally involved movement across the border with Saudi Arabia. Some of these tribes settled in northern villages, while others – though persisting in Saudi Arabia – cross to Qatar for no more than the grazing of camels in the south of the country.

Nomads carry the minimum. There was scant place for the non-essential. Camels were used as pack animals, to provide meat and milk. Their hair (the tough outer coat and soft undercoat) was used together with goat hair and sheep's wool to weave fabric for tents, mats, dividers, bags and clothes. The craft skills survive today even if the way of life does not.

Camel produce still provides goods for trading. Camels can be milked anything up to six times a day; at peak production, the daily yield from a 400kg animal is around 15 litres. Milk is produced for nine to eighteen months after foaling. The meat is rich in protein but not a high energy source, so anything in excess of the families' needs was traded in town for grain. It was the women who tended the animals, and also who took the produce to market, together with their handicrafts, establishing themselves as skilful traders.

The traditional brown-and-black and cream Bedouin tents, the *Bayt Al Shahr* (House of Hair) were tightly woven in sections, incorporating goat hair which produced a wind-proof, waterproof shelter for the nomadic families. At each new location, the women would erect the tents, sewing the panels together. At the end of their stay they would reverse the process, packing away the tents and loading them onto the camels. Lighter weight coloured panels were used to divide the tent into rooms or sections – one for

knives or later large scissors, and the hair was sorted by hand to remove grit and debris – but not washed – before being carded to align the fibres. A long thin spindle was used to create the tough and highly-twisted yarn; hair was selected according to the end use of the fabric to be woven. Originally desert plants and minerals were used to create the dyes – mainly red and orange – but latterly, chemical dyes have played their part.

For the weaving itself, the weft yarn was wound round a shuttle, *al misha*. A gazelle horn,

Desert hospitality has turned the preparation of coffee into something of a ritual, traditionally conducted by the men. The first step is the roasting of the beans over a hot fire.

the men, another for the women. Extensions functioned as kitchens or to protect the animals.

Accumulations of woven items were seen as reflections of the status and wealth of the owner. Outworn items were discarded to lighten the burden, so few really old pieces now remain. (Cushion covers are a recent innovation.) Weaving was the job of women, and remains so at craft centres. The skills passed from mother to daughter. They set up simple horizontal looms outside the tent, creating fabric in widths of 50-60 cm., and a minimum length of one and a half metres.

Sheep, goats and camels were sheared using

*al qurn,* was used to pick over the threads and make sure they were in the right order, the weaver strumming the horn across the threads.

The generic name given to weaving is *al sadu*, but the term is also applied to the simplest and most popular style of flat-weave. The (vertical) warp threads are closely spaced, and they conceal the weft (horizontal) threads, producing an extremely hard-wearing cloth, known in English as 'warp-face plain weave' with both sides of the fabric having the same appearance. As to design, *hubub* comprises two contrasting warp colours, usually black and white, used as a border pattern with a 'tooth' motif. *Dhalla* is a popular design for cushions, storage bags and rugs which produces fine horizontal stripes giving the fabric a ribbed appearance. The design is worked in bands, and is seen in weaving of wool, wool-and-cotton mix or of goat hair and cotton. *Al Ain* is the Arabic word for an eye, and this pattern is exactly like a white 'eye' on a black background, and is most frequently found in a piece bordered by flatweave. *Uwairjan* is a familiar pattern: a single row of 'spotted' pyramids, either red or white dots on black. *Midkhar* is similar, but more

## Architecture

Modern architecture in Qatar has been influenced by the dwellings of the nomadic and settled populations, and by the formidable and sometimes stylish rulers' forts.

Until modern times, most permanent dwellings were small one room structures built of mud brick, limestone or coral blocks, their roofs constructed of mangrove poles covered with palm frond matting, mud and gypsum. Larger dwellings consisted of several rooms,

mangrove poles – two to three metres. Kitchens were either built outside or as walled-off areas of the main room. Storage niches were built into the walls.

Several deserted villages remain as reminders of the traditional house style, the crumbling surfaces revealing the herring-bone courses of stone work or the sun-dried mud blocks. Except for the rulers and their forts, rich merchants were the only people to have more elaborate houses. Even the larger dwellings were restricted to two storeys. Walls and crenellations around the flat

Self-sufficiency in cooking utensils - of clay and iron and wood - was essential until the importation of mass manufactures in recent times *(above)*. The long-beaked coffee pot – *dallah* – will remain on the fire much of the day *(left)*. Cardamom pods are an essential ingredient.

A raffia weaver uses the product of palm fronds for his materials *(right)*.

complex and worked into a branching pattern. *Dhurus al khail* is the 'horse's tooth' pattern worked in two colours: black with red, white or orange. The most complex pattern – and the last one to be mastered by the women as they learned their craft – was *Shajarah* (tree): separate rectangles, each containing a separate design which could be abstract geometric shapes, incorporate writing or include animal motifs. Frequently-used designs were the *wasm* (literally meaning 'spot'), the brands used to mark ownership of the livestock.

Many of the styles and patterns are common throughout the Gulf.

side-by-side without connecting doors, but each with a door leading out onto a covered verandah, sometimes around a courtyard. Blank walls formed the back of the house, protecting it from the prevailing gusty and dusty *shamal*. The small unglazed windows, shaded verandahs (*lewan*) which kept sunlight off the doors, and the thick walls combined to keep the interiors dark and cool in summer, but warm in winter. Timber was scarce; doors and shutters were valuable commodities which moved with the owners if they moved house. The depth of each room or verandah was determined by the average length of the

roof were practical considerations, since beds would be set out on the roof in the hotter months to catch the night-time breezes. Larger houses would sometimes be built around a central courtyard, with boundary walls and entrance gateways designed to provide privacy.

Large wooden gateways were often inset with a smaller arched postern gate, requiring the visitor simultaneously to crouch a little and step over the lower beam of the main door as he entered.

Gates opened in such a way as to screen the living quarters from without. These quarters were made elegant by the open-worked

The sophistication of much of the country's modern architecture derives from Qatar's ancient buildings which have been scrupulously preserved. The spare elegance of the former Palace of Qatar (*right*) recalls the dignity and taste of a former age.

The presence in Qatar of plentiful gypsum has allowed for the development of intricate panelling in the style of the *mushrabiyya* wooden screen (*above*).

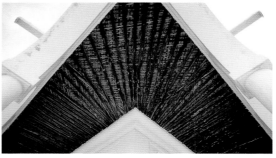

The pointed arch and the woven ceiling (*left*) are characteristics of Qatar's lordly and sacred buildings.

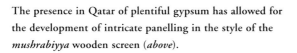

 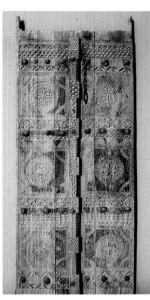  

In the older dwellings of Qatar, it was the wooden doorway that allowed the craftsman to display his skills and inventiveness. Today such surviving doorways (*above*) are carefully preserved and honoured.

reticulated wooden screens – *mushrabiyya* – which served to break the sunlight and admit what breeze there might be. The wind-tower, *badjir*, may be seen as a pre-cursor of air conditioning: a structure which encouraged the natural circulation of air. The modern Qatar University buildings feature both wind and light towers.

Today's buildings often incorporate traditional features such as towers, crenellations, verandahs and mangrove-pole or tent-like ceilings. The use of gypsum panelling or glass and concrete panels using old gypsum designs is common; so is the use of an arch of coloured glass over a doorway or window. Modern wood craftsmen, often from Asia, have recreated the elaborate carved doors, windows and screens, and reproductions of traditional artefacts are often used to enhance the interior decor.

Gypsum was used to finish the walls, and carved gypsum panels decorated the larger buildings. Although the mineral is found and used throughout the Gulf, Qatari gypsum was regarded as being of particularly high quality. The lumps of gypsum were heaped into large kilns, burnt, and then crumbled into a powder. It was then mixed with water in large pits and mixed thoroughly until it reached a thick and creamy texture. It could then be used to plaster walls, seal roofs or, like plaster of Paris, be poured into sand or wood moulds and left to dry. To create intricate decorative panels, the gypsum carver must be able to gauge the correct stage at which to embark on work, using compasses to create the designs which are then carefully cut. If the gypsum is too dry, it is impossible to carve; if it is too damp it will simply crumble to the touch. An uncompleted work will be covered with a damp cloth to retain the correct degree of moisture.

Now, the craftsmen use their skills to create souvenirs for the tourists, and participate in national exhibitions overseas.

## Costume

Whatever they may choose to wear when they relax at home or work out in the numerous fitness clubs around town, Qataris choose modest national dress when they are in public. In summertime, the men wear the long *thobe* or dishdasha, cut along the lines of a shirt which reaches to the ground. It is a matter of pride that their *thobes* should be immaculate, and each man will have his clothes tailor-made, choosing from a vast array of fabric bolts in different shades of white, of different fibres or weaves. Individuality is expressed in the shape of the collar, the buttons and the cuffs. Each Gulf State tends to favour one particular cut, but in modern times many young men will select a style to suit their taste. The *thobe* is worn over long white cotton trousers, or boxer-style shorts. In the cooler winter months, the style of the *thobe* will be the same, but the weight of the fabric increases, and greys, blues and browns make their appearance. To cover their heads, the young Qatari boys wear an embroidered or crotcheted skull cap called a *taqieh*. At first, they will only cover that with the folded square of cloth, the *ghutrah,* for special occasions; later they will wear it on a regular

basis. Snowy white for the summer months, often red-and-white or black-and-white check for the winter, sometimes creamy cashmere patterned in green or black on the corners, the *ghutrah* is held in place with a double black coil, the *iqal* – sometimes with one or two long cords and tassels – which the Bedouin used to use to hobble their camels at night, the loops being pulled over the camel's knee to bend one leg and prevent it moving fast. For ceremonial occasions, the thobe is covered by a thin cream, brown or black gold-edged cloak, the *bisht*. In winter months, a heavy camel hair or wool cloak, the *fahrwa*, often lined with lambswool was worn; in milder weather, it would be replaced by a fleece or wool sleeveless waistcoat. Now, it is becoming more common to see a western-style hunting jacket or a padded anorak!

Older women, following tradition, wear a long dress or *djelabia*, covered when they go out by a black cloak called *abbayah* made from silk, cotton, or a silk and cotton mix. The *djelabia*, often of cotton, are embroidered at the neck and cuffs, and worn over baggy ankle-length trousers called *sirwal*, heavily emboidered around the ankle cuff. More recently, the loose cloak has been

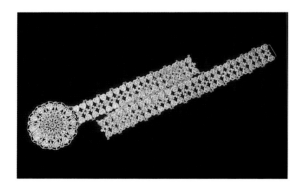

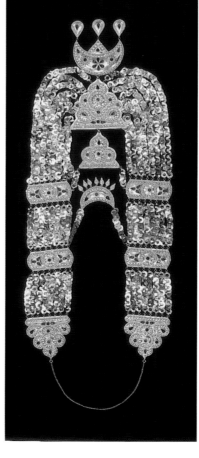

Weddings and family celebrations bring out the exquisite gold jewellery of the women. Illustrated *here* and *opposite* are hairpieces, necklaces, bracelets and pendants - wrought and designed not only for their elegance but in some cases for the bringing of good fortune.

replaced by a tie-fronted cloak or a coat-dress, still in black, and the *djelabia*, whilst remaining the preferred dress of the elderly women, has been replaced for the younger generation by more western dresses or suits – still with long skirts in public, but with up-to-the-minute lengths and designs when worn at home, or at a ladies-only gathering. Qatari women also cover their hair, either with a gossamer-thin scarf called *shaila*, sometimes decorated with silver flecks under a head-to-toe *abbaya*, or with an opaque headscarf. Whilst the older and more traditional women use a short nose or chin-length mask, the *battula*, the younger women, if veiled, generally choose the Bedouin-style chest-length veil, the *burqah*, which just leaves their eyes exposed. Although the masks are made of calico, with match-stick stiffeners over the nose area, they are dyed with indigo, and beaten, giving them a metallic appearance. Young girls, especially on festive occasions, wear the *bukhnoq*, a lightweight black head covering which is chest-length at the front, floor length at the back, heavily embroidered with gold or silver thread around the face and down the centre front panel. Whilst electing to dress modestly in public according to the dictates of their religion, Qatari women nevertheless follow fashion – and parrallel to western designer fashions, the Bedouin veil is a fashion which emerged in the 1990s along with the use of thick black gloves and socks.

Traditional embroidery, by women for women, decorated the intricately patterned *thobe al nashl*, a filmy overdress of lightweight chiffon stitched from vertical and horizontal panels to create a stubby 'T' shaped dress when laid flat. The intricately embroidered *thobe al nashl* was worn by Qatari brides. The ladies-only party in the bride's home – 'henna-night' – is today part of the wedding ritual for a Qatari bride. Exquisite patterns in henna are applied to the hands, arms, feet and ankles of the bride and those (females) closest to her – traditionally by one another, but latterly, often, in beauty parlours.

Nowadays, many of the fine dresses are mass-produced, freehand machine embroidery being used for the the bulk of the gold or silver threadwork, but with beads, pearls, sequins or metallic flakes added by hand. The neck opening and the whole of the centre-front panel of the dress are decorated, whilst the back is left plain, and the wide sleeves can be drawn back and over the head to cover the hair.

Dazzling embroidery characterises the *thobe al nashl* worn by Qatari brides. Such *thobes* and *djelabia* are passed from generation to generation.

65

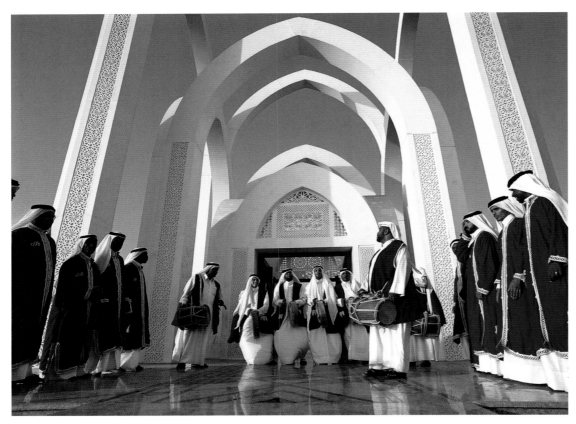

## Dance

The most popular and enduring of dances – and the one performed most frequently at weddings and celebrations – is the *ardha,* described at the end of Chapter 2. Men and women perform separate dances, women dancing only in front of women. However the *lewa* – which originated in East Africa – is one of just two which were originally performed in Qatar by mixed groups. Together with the symbolic *rezif,* the *lewa* is also seen on ceremonial occasions. *Tamboura* (which takes its name from the predominant musical instrument accompanying the dance) was probably brought to Qatar from Africa in the early days of slave trading. *Habban,* on the other hand, came to Qatar with the migrants from the shores of what is now Iran and is performed regularly at weddings and during religious festivals by communities of Iranian origin.

The *fareissa* is unusual because it mimics classical dance by telling a story, the battle between good and evil, the former represented by a hobby horse. Another Gulf dance, it was also performed in the courts of Mediaeval Spain. *Qaderi* and *zaari* are very old, and rather different to other Qatari dances in that they are spiritual in nature, *zaari* in particular having been performed in the hopes of alleviating psychological illnsses.

Many popular dances are performed by groups, but *zafan* is a solo dance by a male performer who is surrounded by a seated circle of singers who provide the beat with clapping and simple percussion instruments. When the dancer jumps in front of one of the singers, they must mirror his movements.

Of the women's dances, *khammary* is performed by a group of masked women at a wedding, whilst *shek sheka* is a much more modern girls' dance which retains aspects of traditional dance but with steps and a tempo which show a degree of western influence.

As for music, we have already referred to the part it played on the pearling boats. Besides those working songs is a long tradition of desert and seafaring songs. Many of the songs were prayers, and were sung in a set order throughout the day, making up what was called the *fgeiri* cycle; within that, the songs fell into several styles: *bahri, adsani, haddadi, mholfi.*

The short-rhythm-cycle *labuni* styles, which characterise so much of Qatar's 'desert' music, are said to have their origins in Kuwait, whilst the *hammari* style folk songs have both desert and coastal versions. Whenever large groups gathered in the evening, whether bedouin or pearl divers, they would sing songs in the *samari* style, designed for thirty or so singers. *Ardah* and *rezif,* besides being dances, are also classified as songs.

Percussion was the invariable accompaniment. The most important instrument for the pearl fishermen was the *gahlah,* a tall clay jar of up to a metre in height, from which the percussionist extracted two notes. Slapping the full palm resoundingly over the neck of the jar produces a bass note; hitting the side of the neck produces the treble sound. *Tus* or *tasat,* the tin drinking cups, were also used as percussion instruments, alongside the more conventional *tabl,* the long drum with skins at either end, suspended from a strap around the player's neck, and beaten with a short stout stick.

Modern performances of the old songs often also include the *tar,* a large tambourine-style instrument not originally taken to sea. Heat raises its pitch. A small double skinned drum, the *murwas* requires much dexterity to play well. Clapping is always sharp and crisp.

Another old percussion 'instrument', frequently featured in the desert music, was made from a string of animal hooves. Modern renditions of old songs feature not just percussion, but strings, in the form of the *oud,* an instrument not far removed from the lute. Visiting western lutists have often improvised alongside the Qatari Folkloric Troupe in concerts.

Festivities bring out people in their traditional finery –
including musicians (*right and opposite*). The age-old
Spring Festival *(above)* has recently been revived; greenery is
symbolicaly cast into the sea to bring fertility and the
prospect of a good yield for the fishermen.

# 5 Islam

The majority of Qataris are Sunni Muslims, adherents of the reforming movement associated with the 18th century Sheikh Mohammed bin Abd al Wahhab of the Najd of central Arabia. This *Muwahhidun* influence has control. Moderation, practicality and balance are guarantees of high integrity and sound morality. Islam recognises the prophets of Judaism and Christianity (called the religions and peoples of the Book), but the Prophet was revealed to the Prophet Mohammed, untainted by any additions. Religious scholars also quote from the *Sunna* (rules), the guidelines of the religion given in the words and actions of the Prophet during his life, and from the Hadith

Islam took Qatar very soon, and emphatically, after the revelation by the Holy Prophet of his Message. Qatar treasures a collection of early illuminated Quranic manuscripts.

been a guiding and stabilising factor in Qatar's modern evolution. Religious *mores* form the basis of the social structure, and the principal ground of legislation is Shari'a or Islamic law, broadly in the Hanbali interpretation.

In Islam, Qataris share their Faith with over 1 billion believers worldwide – roughly one fifth of the world's population. Islam acknowledges Allah as the one and only God and Creator, source of all that is good, true and beautiful. The believer's basic responsibility is to Him; all human beings are the agents of Allah, who created everything in their service. He is wise, just and merciful and does not hold people responsible for those things beyond their

Mohammed is the supreme interpreter of the will of Allah. The Prophet's name is seldom mentioned without an invocation of peace on his behalf.

In the early 7th century AD, the Prophet Mohammed called on the people of Makkah (Mecca) to turn away from paganism and idolatry and worship instead the one true God. An orphan of the Quraysh tribe, which condemned corruption and the ill treatment of women, he was threatened by the Makkans for his preaching and migrated with his followers to Medina, where Islam first began to take hold.

The Holy Book of Islam is the Qur'an, regarded as the true word of God, exactly as it

– the body of tradition about Mohammed and his followers. Sunni Muslims, who are in the majority in the Arabian Gulf, are those who recognise the Sunna; the Shi'ite Muslims (from the Arabic word *sha'a,* to follow), who form the majority in Iran, meanwhile regard the prophet's cousin, Ali, as the rightful successor to the authority of the Holy Prophet and the interpretation of his Message. It is the duty of all Muslims to study and understand the Qur'an. Also it is a source of pride to learn the Qur'an by heart. Islamic studies feature in the curricula of all state schools in Qatar and all Arabic-medium private schools, and are available in many of the expatriate private schools.

Qatar's children also participate with pride in a number of regular Qur'an recitation competitions.

Islam stresses the acquisition of knowledge and education; it also regards all people as equal in the eyes of God – which is not to say identical: equal in the sense that they come into this word free from sin and with no material possessions and that they will take nothing material with them when they die; non-identical in that they each have their own separate talents and skills. Islam encourages respect for others, particularly for women and for the elderly.

exercise of that will through work and personal dedication.

The religious duties of the Muslim are premised upon what are known as the Five Pillars of Islam:

- the *Shahadatayn* or Oral Confession: 'There is no God but God, and Mohammed is His prophet';
- the duty to pray five times a day: at dawn, midday, afternoon, sunset and before retiring for the night;
- the requirement to fast during the holy month of Ramadan;

Mohammed is His Prophet. Whether the *muezzin* climbs the steps of the minaret to make the call, or remains at the base to broadcast the call through microphones, it is ensured that the call is heard by the Faithful. It is open to any of the devout to call his fellows to prayer: he may or may not be the Imam. The Imams, however, of any community in Qatar will have studied the *Shari'a* at an institute of learning. The role of Imam will often run in a family.

Qatar's mosques vary in size, in the shape of their minarets, and in the design of their space for worship. Around the country are to be found

Friday prayer packs the mosques of the country – as here at that of Abu Bakr al Sidiq in Doha.

From the personal greeting of 'As-salaam Aleykum', 'Peace be Upon You', to the welcome for a newborn infant or the utterances of condolence expressed at the time of a death, the formularies of the Faith occur throughout daily life. Each act or formal speech is prefaced with the words which open the Qur'an, 'Bismillah ur-Rahman-ur-Rahim' – 'In the name of God, the compassionate, the Merciful'. Every promise or expectation voiced will be prefaced by the word 'Inshallah' – 'God Willing' – since everything which comes to pass in this world does so only subject to the will of Allah. That is not to imply any fatalism. Islam gives thanks for God's gift of free will, and encourages the

- the duty to offer *zakat* or alms to the poor, to the value of 2.5 per cent of surplus income;
- the duty for each person to try to perform Hajj – the pilgrimage to Makkah – at least once during a lifetime.

The call to prayer echoes out from the minarets of Qatar's many mosques at each prayer time. In a city like Doha, its mounting call can be heard from every side, the voices of the *muezzin* varying in tone and clarity, each with the same words, beginning: *Allahu Akbar, Allahu Akbar, Ash-shadu an la illah illa Allah; Mohammed Rasoul Allah*: God is Great, God is Great, There is no God but God, and

tiny old mosques sufficient for a mere handful of prayer-goers, or simple prefabricated structures used on a temporary basis, or rural mosques with solar-panels to generate their own electricity, or majestic and beautiful town mosques. Open spaces are consecrated for prayer at festivals.

Friday is the Muslim holy day, with congregational prayers held at midday. On that occasion, in addition to the normal prayers, the Imam will deliver a sermon (*khutbah*) from a pulpit, or *minbar*. During the week, many will say their prayers at home or in the office. Travellers will still stop by the wayside wherever they happen to be at prayer time, carefully unfolding their prayer mat to lay it on the ground for the coming statutory obeisances. Prayers are said facing the Kaaba in Makka al Mukarramah are preceded by the performance of a very defined set of the ablutions, and *Wodhu,* which require the washing of the hands and arms to the elbows, the feet, the face and nostrils. Each mosque has a special area where such cleansing is performed. Where several people pray together, they will form a straight line, shoulder to shoulder, with one person in front leading the prayer.

have both *Forood* mosques, where all except Friday prayers are performed, and *Jumma* mosques, where all prayers including Friday prayers are held.

There are over 1060 mosques in Qatar, spread across the country's ten municipalities. The construction of new mosques is overseen by the Ministry of Awqafs and Islamic Affairs. Sometimes wealthy citizens will finance the construction of a mosque near their home in service to the local community, or

eating, drinking, smoking or physical intercourse from dawn until dusk. In practice, many men will refrain even from shaking hands with a woman during the fasting hours of Ramadan.

Daytime Ramadan begins just before dawn: according to the Qur'an, from that moment at which it is possible to distinguish a white thread from a black one. It continues until sunset: religious authorities specify in advance the exact moment.

Wakrah declares its spiritual authority by night with the aid of floodlights (*above and left*).

In busy market areas, the faithful often gather in too large a number to fit inside the small mosques; instead they will line up outside the mosque, on the pavement or open ground, join in the prayer. To walk immediately in front of someone saying prayers can negate those prayers, so individuals or groups will try to position themselves facing a wall in a secluded area and passers-by will move behind them.

In order to ensure that everyone can comfortably reach their nearest mosque on foot to say their prayers, each neighbourhood will

dedicated to the name of a deceased relative.

The Islamic calendar began in the year the Prophet Mohammed migrated from Makka to Medina in 622 AD. It follows the lunar months, and the year is consequently 11 days shorter than the Gregorian (Western) calendar year. Ramadan, which is the ninth month of the Hijra calendar, therefore falls earlier in each successive year according to the Gregorian calendar. It commemorates the month in which God revealed the holy Qur'an to Mohammed, and all Moslems are expected to refrain from

To help the faithful observe the correct fasting period, Qatar's armed forces man cannons placed around towns which fire blanks at the precise starting and finishing times. Children and families nowadays gather to watch the cannon being fired at sunset before they go home to break their fast – traditionally with dates and water, before gathering for a family meal, *Iftar.* The only people exempt from fasting are young children, the sick, those requiring oral medication or whose health would be damaged by fasting, those travelling long distances, women who are menstruating and women who have just given birth. The fast is only obligatory from the age of puberty, but younger children are encouraged to fast on occasional days from the age of seven or under. Adults unable to fast on certain days are required to make up those days at a later time. Fasting is considered to be good physically and spiritually, as a means of cleansing the body of toxins and of encouraging self-discipline.

Qatar's restaurants, cafés and juice stalls close

into the night. Around 2 a.m. or 3 a.m., those fasting will have a last meal (*sahour*), often waking specially for the occasion.

In the middle of the month Qatari children celebrate Ramadan in their own way with *Garangou*, visiting neighbourhood houses in groups to sing traditional songs and receiving, in return, sweets which they collect in white linen shoulder bags as they go. Ramadan is a time when tolerance and understanding are emphasised, and fighting is frowned upon unless

holiday people will visit their closest relatives as well as their neighbours. The men will also pay their respects and re-pledge their allegiance in person to the Emir. Families prepare fine meals to regale their guests.

At the end of the pilgrimage month of *Dhul Al Hijjah*, Muslims celebrate *Eid Al Adha*, ('Big Eid'), the Feast of Sacrifice which follows the Hajj or pilgrimage to Makkah. No longer do pilgrims journey across continents on foot to reach the holy sites. Most now travel by bus or

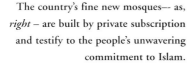
The country's fine new mosques— as, *right* – are built by private subscription and testify to the people's unwavering commitment to Islam.

during the day in Ramadan. Hotels keep just one restaurant open for their non-Muslim guests. In the late afternoon, they begin to prepare the food to serve at *Iftar,* or for people to take away. There are special dishes prepared during Ramadan, and families will prepare extra food, delivering savoury and sweet delicacies to their neighbours. Small food stalls appear specially for Ramadan, serving kebabs, samosas and special sweets; shops change their timings, often opening in the morning but then not again until after sunset and staying open late

in national defence or in defence of the Faith.

The month begins and ends with the sighting of the new moon (moon-sighting committees are appointed to oversee the announcements) and Ramadan is followed by the feast of *Eid Al Fitr* ('Little Eid'). It is a religious occasion, when dawn prayers are held in the Friday mosques or in huge open-air prayer grounds. But Eid is also a family occasion. New clothes are bought by those who can afford them, and charities hand out new garments to the needy. Gifts are exchanged, and on the first day of the three-day

by plane in organised groups. Yet other aspects of Hajj remain as they did hundreds of years ago. The faithful performing Hajj – who earn the title *Hajji* – wear a simple white garment (*ihram*), made from a single seamless piece of material; and the women, though covering their hair, leave their faces unveiled.

First, on reaching Makkah, they walk seven times around the Ka'aba, then seven times between the hills of Safa and Manwah. That commemorates the search for water by Hagar, who ran back and forth to find water for her thirsty son, Ismail – a quest which came to an end when God opened a spring at the site of the well of Zamzam. Next, they walk to Mount Arafah, with ritual halts (*waqf*). On the way to the valley of Mina, they stop to throw stones at vertical rocks at Jamrat Al Aqabah, symbolically stoning the devil. On the pilgrims' return to Mina, a camel (or more commonly a sheep, goat or other horned animal) is sacrificed for *Eid Al Adha*. Before discarding the *ihram* and resuming secular dress, the *hajjis* will shave their heads.

way. Recognising both the financial and emotional demands of these injunctions, fewer and fewer Qatari men are now taking more than one wife.

According to Islam, the Muslim woman has the same right to education as the man – a right emphatically upheld in today's Qatar, where (for instance) the majority of students at Qatar's universities are women. Marriage is regarded as a partnership in which the man must take ultimate responsibility for providing for the family; and

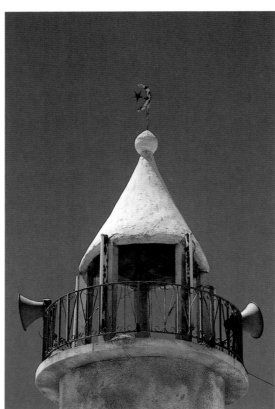

Every town and village has its own spiritual centre or centres, proclaimed by the minarets, such as that of touching simplicity at Fuwairat (*left*).

In Islam women are honoured and valued in their own right, as mothers and as nurturers of the next generation. While Islam permits polygamy, it does not promote it. The practice was permitted in order to ensure that in times of conflict, when many men were killed in battle, widows could re-marry and thus find the protection and shelter which might otherwise be denied to them. But the Qur'an is quite clear than no man should take more than one wife unless he can guarantee to treat them equally both spiritually and materially - nor should he have a favourite, or treat wives differently in any

women must give their consent before being committed to an arranged marriage. Women also retain their own names after marriage, rather than taking the family name of their husband. They have the right to own property, to manage their finances or real estate, to sign documents or engage in legal transactions relating to their property, to act as a trustee or establish a business. They have rights of inheritance and the right to work outside the home and to go out into the community. If she chooses to have a career, the Muslim woman's religion says simply that she should not put it before, or let it seriously interfere with, her role as wife and mother. Women may be appointed to public offices – as evidenced recently, for instance, by a woman taking a seat on Doha's Water Board. Qatar vigorously upholds Islam's precept of the equal value of women and men, personally and spiritually.

Family disputes, questions of inheritance, of morality, and cases of marital breakdown are dealt with by the Shari'a Courts. Shari'a law is based on the Qur'an, the Sunna and Hadith,

widows and orphans, and the education of non-Muslims in the Faith through the Depatment of Daw'a or Enlightenment. If a Qatari woman loses 'her father and has no husband, then responsibility for her care rests with her nearest male relative, as her guardian.

Islam requires both men and women to dress modestly. The women are expected to cover their hair in public, and to wear loose fitting clothes which leave only their hands and feet exposed. Qatari national dress meets the requirements,

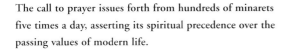

The call to prayer issues forth from hundreds of minarets five times a day, asserting its spiritual precedence over the passing values of modern life.

*Ijma* (the consensus of the Ulema or religious scholars regarding matters not dealt with explicitly in the Qur'an) and finally *Qiyas* – reasoning based on analogy with reference to the other sources.

Male and female students study Shari'a separately at Qatar University, as they do with all other subjects. Most of the women graduates from that department subsequently join either the Ministry of Education and Higher Education to teach Islamic studies in schools, or the Ministry of Endowments (*Awqafs*) and Islamic Affairs. The Ministry also oversees provisions for

while also providing a way of protecting the skin from the fierce sunlight. Visitors to Qatar are not encouraged to don local dress, but are expected to observe the cultural norms. Women, therefore, should not wear excessively short skirts or shorts – except to swim or in the relative privacy of a hotel swimming area. It is preferable for women to cover their shoulders, and to avoid plunging necklines. Equally men are expected to restrict the wearing of shorts in public places, and not to go about shirtless. Observance of dress codes by non-Muslims is considered particularly important during Ramadan.

# 6 Government

'Dawlat Qatar', the State of Qatar, has existed as an independent entity since the late 1800s, and has been ruled by the Al Thani family since then.

Al Thani were among a tribal group which settled for a long time at Gebrin oasis in southern Najd before their arrival in Qatar during the early 18th century. Initially they stayed in the north of the peninsula before moving to Doha in the mid 19th century under the leadership of Mohammed Bin Thani.

The family of Al Thani is a branch of the Arab tribe Tamim, whose descent is traced back to Mudar Bin Nizar. This tribe inhabited the eastern parts of the Arabian peninsula.

The name of Al Thani is derived from that of the family's ancestor Thani Bin Mohammed, father of Mohammed bin Thani who was the first sheikh to rule over the Qatar peninsula during the mid 19th century.

The current Emir, HH Sheikh Hamad Bin Khalifa Al Thani, is the eighth member of the family to have ruled the country, the leadership having passed on five times in that period before the death of the previous ruler but with the support of the ruling family.

The previous Al Thani rulers and period of reign were: Mohammed Bin Thani Al Thani, 1850-1878; Qassim Bin Mohammed Al Thani, 1878-1913; Abdullah Bin Qassim Bin Mohammed Al Thani, 1913-1949 (1913 is usually quoted as the beginning of his rule, but he actually assumed the leadership in 1905 during his father's lifetime); Hamad Bin Abdullah Al Thani, 1940-1948 – de facto ruler during his father's latter years, although just outlived by Abdullah; Ali Bin Abdullah Bin Qassim Al Thani, 1949-1960 (abdicated); Ahmed Bin Ali Bin Abdullah Al Thani, 1960-1972; Khalifa Bin Hamad Bin Abdullah Al

The national flag has become a symbol of Qatar's emergence as an influential Islamic state. The seated edge of the deep purple (the original dye being obtained from ancient times from marine molusc *murex*) is reminiscent of the crenellations characteristic of Qatari defensive architecture: it is a unique and striking feature among the flags of the world.

The evolution of the Advisory Council – seen in session here (*above left*) – into an elected parliament as the central legislative body in twenty-first century Qatar, is known to be favoured by HH the Emir (*above*), who has led the initiative for constitutional development in Qatar.

Doha's famous clock tower (*below*), erected in the 1960s, is a part of the capital's image of good order. Under HH the Emir and the Ministry of Foreign Affairs (left) the State has achieved an unprecedented level of international recognition.

The Emir's Palace in Doha, commanding the waterfront, is not so much a royal residence as the pivotal structure of modern government.

Thani, 1972 -1995. Sheikh Khalifa (born 1932) assumed power with the support of the ruling family as did Hamad Bin Khalifa Al Thani, who succeeded in 1995.

Sheikh Hamad, who was born in Doha in 1950, undertook both his primary and secondary education in Qatar before joining Britain's prestigious Sandhurst Academy, graduating from there in 1971. It is a tradition which has been echoed in the training of his brother, the Prime Minister H.H. Sheikh Abdullah Bin Khalifa Al Thani, and Sheikh Hamad's third and fourth sons, H.H. Sheikh Jassem Bin Hamad Al Thani and H.H the

Heir Apparent Sheikh Tamim Bin Hamad Al Thani.

Following his graduation Sheikh Hamad joined the Qatari Armed Forces with the rank of Lieutenant Colonel, and was appointed commander of the First Mobile Regiment, which now bears his name. It was the beginning of a career which saw his promotion to Major-General and then to the post of Commander-in-Chief of the Armed Forces in 1972. He was appointed both Heir Apparent and Minister of Defence in 1977. Two years later, recognising the importance of developing Qatar's Youth, he took on the Chairmanship of the Higher

Council for Youth Welfare. He has continued to give support to youth and sports activities, and has stressed the fundamental role of education in preparing the country to face the challenges of the new millennium.

In 1989, he took on the Chairmanship of the Higher Council for Planning, laying the cornerstone for the modern state which exists today. As Heir Apparent, he became increasingly involved in major policy-making decisions and gradually took over the reins of government, so that when he assumed power on 27 June 1995, he already had a vision for the future which would modernise the state, develop its economic potential, and increase the number of nationals actively involved in the government and private sectors at all levels.

One of the first Decrees issued by Sheikh Hamad was that governing the rules of accession in the State. Sheikh Jassem was appointed Heir Apparent on October 26th 1996, with this role passing to his younger brother Sheikh Tamim on 5 August 2003. Following the constitutional separation of the role of Emir and Prime Minister, Sheikh Hamad's second brother, Abdullah, was appointed Premier on 29 October 1996. On 16 September 2003 in a re-shuffle, H.E. Sheikh Hamad Bin Jassim Bin Jabr Al-Thani was appointed First Deputy Prime Minister and Minister of Foreign Affairs, and HE Abdullah Bin Hamad Al-Attiyah as Second Deputy Prime Minister and Minister of Energy and Industry.

In mid-2000, a 32-member high level committee, formed on the instruction of the Emir in July 1999, started drafting a new constitution for the country, which contained provisions for an elected assembly. On 2 July 2002 the manuscript was submitted to the Emir. A public referendum was held on 29 April 2003 which approved adoption of the constitution with nearly 97% approval. The Emir ratified the new constitution on 8 June 2004 and it came into force on 9 June 2005. The constitution allows for free speech, a free press and freedom of assembly "according to the law," but does not allow for the formation of political parties and stipulates that no changes can be made to the document for the first 10 years it is in effect.

The Emir is designated as Head of State, rule being hereditary within the Al Thani family. He is assisted by the Council of Ministers (Cabinet) in consultation with the 35-member Advisory Council appointed by an Emiri decision. The Advisory Council elects a Speaker and Deputy Speaker by secret ballot and proportional majority, (not fewer than half the council's members plus one). It debates the State's general policy in political, economic and administrative matters (including the draft budget), and social and cultural affairs, and refers its recommendations to the cabinet.

The Council of Ministers is required to prepare a comprehensive plan for all aspects of State development, and to propose draft laws and statutes to that end, supervising their subsequent implementation and those of the courts. It is responsible for setting up and monitoring government departments and agencies, supervising the protection of State interests abroad and the creation of systems necessary to uphold State security and public order at home.

Sheikh Hamad has made it clear that he wants to spread the democratic experience, which started with the election of a 29-member Central Municipal Council in March 1999 on a four-year term. New elections were held in April 2003. Women were registered both as voters and candidates for those elections and will also be eligible for future parliamentary elections. While the Council initially has had an advisory role, it was expected to assume executive authority at a later stage. The profile of Qatari women has been raised dramatically both at home and abroad through the active encouragement of the Emir's wife, HH Sheikha Moza Bint Nasser Al Misnad, who is President of the Supreme Council for Family Affairs which reports directly to the Cabinet. Her deputy, Sheikha Hessa Bint Khalifa bin Hamad Al Thani, is one of an increasing number of Qatari women to hold the rank of Undersecretary within the government.

In other moves to open up the country and foster democracy, the Emir lifted censorship of the local press in October 1995, and in 1998 the Ministry of Information was disbanded. The work of the ministry was re-assigned to other ministries and independent organisations. In 1996, the Emir issued a decree amending the statutes of the Qatar Chamber of Commerce and Industry, so as to ensure the election of members of the Board of Directors by direct vote.

In June 2000, Qatar's Cabinet took the decision to re-organise certain aspects of its structure, at the same time taking steps to issue a law forming the Qatar Electricity and Water Corporation. A reallocation and re-organisation of the responsibilities for the generation and distribution of electricity and desalinated water in the country between the Qatar Electricity and Water Company and the Qatar Electricity and Water Corporation was expected to lead to the dissolution of the Ministry of Electricity and Water, which latterly was held as a joint portfolio by the Minister of Energy and Industry in the Cabinet.

While defence falls under the direct orders of the Emir in his role as Commander-in Chief of the Armed Forces. other portfolios represented in Cabinet are; Foreign Affairs; Finance; Economy and Commerce; Awqafs (Endowments) and Islamic Affairs; Municipal

Recent years have seen the emergence of Qatar not only on the regional international stage but, indeed, globally. This is exemplified by the significance accorded by world powers to State and official visits by His Highness the Emir - seen here in the company of Her Majesty Queen Elizabeth II of Britain (*above*).

In Sarajevo, capital of Bosnia, His Highess the Emir is seen here with the members of the joint presidency of the war-torn fellow Muslim state. Momcilo Krajisnik (*left*), Kresimir Zubak (*right*), and Alija Izetbegovic to the left of the Emir. Qatar increased its financial support for reconstruction.

His Highness the Emir is seen here meeting President Chirac of France (*below*) and inspecting a unit of the Brigade of Guards on arrival in London, accompanied by HRH Prince Philip (*opposite*).

Affairs and Agriculture; Civil Service Affairs and Housing; Energy and Industry; Education; and Justice.

The Ministry of Civil Service Affairs and Housing oversees the recruitment, employment and remuneration policies in government ministries and departments. It also receives, evaluates and approves, as appropriate, interest free loans for Qatari nationals to build their own houses on land donated by the government. It also provides low-cost housing to Qataris from the lower income groups. Aware of the cost effectiveness and efficiency resulting from the introduction of sound administrative policies, the ministry also oversees the functioning of the Administrative Development Training Centre.

As Minister of Defence and Supreme Commander of the Armed Forces, the Emir has ensured the full development and modernisation of the country's land, sea and air forces. Striving for excellence, the armed forces participate in regular joint exercises with those of the other Gulf Co-operation Council States and friendly countries with which Qatar has defence agreements. As with other Gulf States, Qatar has purchased military equipment from a wide variety of sources, preferring not to be

dependent on any one country or supplier for its needs. Armed Forces personnel undertake regular training both at home and overseas in order to familiarise themselves with the most up-to-date thinking and techniques. The defensive powers of the country's military were also used to great effect in support of allied forces during the 1991 activities to liberate Kuwait.

Internal Security is guaranteed by the Ministry of Interior. The Department of Public Security has several different specialised sections. The department of immigration, passport and nationality deals with the issuance of passports, travel documents, visas, residence permits and ID cards, referring applications for naturalisation to a specialised committee. The Traffic and Patrol Department is responsible for the organisation and supervision of traffic, the issuance of driving licences, the imposition of traffic laws and the apprehension of violators, and also for regular street patrols and the general safety of the community. Civil Defence is equipped with advanced fire fighting and rescue equipment, and is responsible for preventing, containing, and eliminating risks. The

**National day provides an occasion for the display of Qatar's land, air and sea forces.**

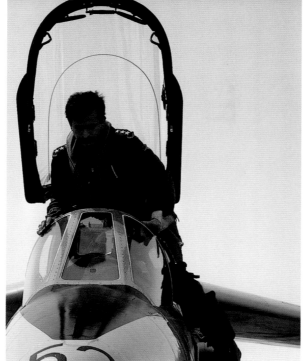

Metropolitan Police (sometimes called Capital Police) are responsible for maintaining security in Doha, including the investigation of crimes and control of security at the air and sea ports. The coastguard department is also part of the Ministry of Interior.

As to foreign policy and world affairs, Qatar is committed to preserving its own national integrity and security, and to promoting the political, economic and social standards of its own society – but not to the detriment of its involvement with the international community. Under the leadership of the Emir, the State has achieved an unprecedented level of international recognition and grown in stature through its pursuit of peace and stability; support for territorial integrity and the legitimate rights of people across the globe and peaceful resolution of conflicts in the region and world wide. The state rejects and condemns ethnic cleansing, all forms of racial discrimination, the suppression of human rights and all forms of terrorism, recognising the need to differentiate between terrorism and the legitimate struggle of people to realise their rights in accordance with the provisions of international law.

Qatar works to establish and maintain close

relations with all peace-loving countries and peoples and is an active member of regional and international bodies in its pursuit of global peace, security and understanding. At the regional level, Qatar has been a member of the Co-operation Council for the Arab States of the Gulf (GCC) since its inception in 1981. Within the framework of the Arab League and the Damascus Declaration it seeks to re-establish the unity of the Arab world on the basis of frankness, objectivity and a realisation of mutual Arab interests. At the Islamic level and through its membership and, from the year 2000, its three-year chairmanship of the Organisation of the Islamic Conference (OIC), it constantly

seeks ways to consolidate ties of co-operation between Islamic peoples and countries.

Qatar has emphasised the need for financial reform of the United Nations, to ensure long-term financial stability for the organisation. It has urged developed countries to meet their financial obligations to the organisation's ordinary budget and towards the financing of peace-keeping operations so that the UN role is not undermined. And with its growing international presence, Qatar has also developed a significant role as a mediator in conflict situations, seeking their resolution through discussion and the patient insistence upon mutual understanding.

Justice and the rule of law are dispensed by the Ministry of Justice (*above left*), the courteous traffic policeman (*top*) and police headquarters (*above*), in a country where the crime rate must surely be one of the lowest in the world.

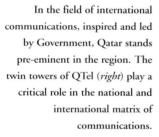

In the field of international communications, inspired and led by Government, Qatar stands pre-eminent in the region. The twin towers of QTel (*right*) play a critical role in the national and international matrix of communications.

# 7 The Economy, Industry & Commerce

It would have been a brave person indeed who would have prophesised at the beginning of the twentieth century that the barren peninsula would become, by the century's close, one of the most modern and dynamic economies of the region.

In the second half of the twentieth century, Qatar transformed itself into an ultra-modern economy with highly developed industries and services using the latest technology and fully integrated into the global economic system. Not only has the nature of the economy changed beyond all recognition but, in considerable measure, the physical appearance of the peninsula also. Modern technology has allowed the development of agriculture, creating oases of greenery in the desert landscape. The Government has used the riches arising from exploitation of Qatar's oil resources to create this economic miracle and place it on a sustainable basis. The development of manufacturing industries based on the country's oil and gas resources and the export of liquefied natural gas (LNG) should ensure the country's prosperity in the twenty-first century and beyond.

As Qatar enters the twenty-first century, its economy is in a strong position and the Qatari business community is poised to take advantage of the emerging commercial opportunities. Oil production, the mainstay of the Qatari economy for 50 years, is at near record levels and new capacity is being brought on-stream as offshore fields are developed and exploration undertaken onshore. The country's oil reserves are not unlimited and will eventually be exhausted. Fortunately, however, Qatar is blessed in addition with some of the world's

*Natural gas is cooled to -160ºC and compressed down to a volume ratio of 600 to 1 in preparation for the journey in these vast LNG tankers, bound here for the Far East.*

Modern desalination plants have enabled irrigation and agriculture on a scale impossible when dependent only on the scant rainfall.

largest natural gas reserves. Natural gas is widely regarded as the fuel of the future and the closing years of the twentieth century saw Qatar export its first LNG shipments to key Asian markets. At the same time, Qatar has developed petrochemical and manufacturing capabilities that take advantage of its abundant hydrocarbon resources to produce chemicals that can be used in many industrial processes. This capability is encouraging the development of companies that turn these chemicals into practical industrial and consumer products. Qatar's economic success is increasingly coming to the attention of the international business community. The Emirate as a whole, and particularly Doha, has evolved as a key regional and international business centre. Doha is now well placed to host important political and

business conferences and exhibitions.

### Agriculture & Water

In Qatar, water is precious. Average annual rainfall is a mere 75mm. This falls mainly between October and March with January the most likely month for rain. The country does, though, experience long periods without any rainfall. The Emirate has only a few underground aquifers and no surface freshwater sources. Qatar is therefore heavily reliant on desalination for its water. The need to provide water for a modern economy has driven investment in modern technology to extract, distribute and use water in the most efficient manner. Three major desalination plants exist – a small one at Ras Abu Aboud and two larger ones at Ras Abu Fontas. Together these supply around 100 million gallons of water per day. In

Modern techniques in agriculture mean that a large proportion of local demand can be supplied from domestic crops (*top and right*). Dates (*above*) have been harvested on the peninsula since ancient times.

2004 the Ras Laffan Power Company Limited's gas driven electricity generation and water desalination plant in Ras Laffan increased that amount by 40% and an extension under construction for completion in 2006 will add a similar volume.

This investment in technology has allowed Qatar to develop a thriving agricultural capacity in the harsh desert conditions. Largely thanks to desalinated water, the Emirate now has 7,000 hectares of arable land and 50,000 hectares of pasturage. Up to the year 2001, there were 916 farms in Qatar, occupying a total area of 60,713 hectares against 650,000 hectares of uncultivated arable lands, and this growth has allowed Qatar to become 70 per cent self-sufficient in summer vegetables and 40 per cent self-sufficient in winter vegetables. The main crops are cereals, tomatoes and other summer produce such as lettuce and cucumber, and fruits. In 1995, cereal production stood at 4,256 metric tonnes. Although this is still far short of the Emirate's needs (around 90,000 tonnes annually), it still marks a significant achievement in a country that has, historically, practised little agriculture. Until very recently, the little agriculture that did occur on the peninsula consisted only of date cultivation. This was coupled with camel rearing and fishing.

## Communications

These days you are likely to arrive in Qatar on board a modern jet belonging to Qatar Airways, pass through formalities at Doha's ultra-modern international airport and then travel by car the short distance into central Doha along a multi-lane highway. Meanwhile you will be able to inform contacts in the city or family back home of your arrival on your GSM-compatible mobile phone, thanks to Q-Tel, the Qatar Telecommunications Company. Once in your hotel room, you will be able to unwind by watching Al-Jazeera television station in Arabic or from December 2005, Al-Jazeera International in English – one of the most innovative and stimulating television channels in the region. If you are importing goods, they will arrive at one of Qatar's three ports, probably Doha port itself or – in the case of oil-related goods – Messaieed. The third port at Ras Laffan is for the gas industry (see below). Such are the high standards of Qatar's communications infrastructure. Qatar has developed a modern and sophisticated communications infrastructure to serve its fast

Qatar Airways is the world's fastest growing airline *(top)*, scheduled to increase its fleet to 56 aircraft by 2011. Its headquarters will move to the new airport (visualisation of the VIP terminal *above left*, and the internal design, *above middle*), which will be one of the biggest in the world, with an annual capacity of 50 million passengers on its completion in 2015.

growing economy. In keeping with its commitment to trade, the Emirate has constructed an integrated network for the import and export of goods and their distribution around the country. A reliable telecommunications network supports its communications infrastructure and allows business to use the latest technology to run operations. Qatari businesses and other organisations, like their counterparts elsewhere, are developing a strong presence on the Internet.

For much of Qatar's history, the main settlements were scattered along the coast and readily accessible only by sea. There was little communication with the peninsula's interior. This has now all changed. Qatar has built a comprehensive road network that links all parts of the Emirate – both coastal and inland. Qatar possesses over 1,100km of paved road, with the network centred naturally on the capital, Doha. Well-maintained dual carriageways link Doha

with Al-Ruwais on the northern tip of the peninsula, Dukhan in the far west, Abu Samra and Sawda Natheel in the far south on the border with Saudi Arabia, and of course with the port of Messaieed south of Doha. In addition, the dual carriageways to Abu Samra and Sawda Natheel integrate Qatar into the regional road network – linking the country with Saudi Arabia and the UAE. These dual carriageways are the backbone of a network of main roads, which serve other important towns such as Ras Laffan, Al Zubara, Al Khor, Al Jumailiyah and Umm Bab.

The completion of a new terminal at Doha International airport early in the twenty-first century will have enhanced Qatar's already first class air services and make a significant contribution to the Emirate's economic development. The new airport has been designed to allow Qatar to fulfil its potential as a regional transport hub for both passengers and

cargo. Qatar is ideally situated to serve as a transit point between Europe and North America on the one hand and Asia on the other as well as providing a conveniently located entry point for the Gulf region. Over twenty international airlines already serve Doha, linking Qatar to virtually every major business centre on every continent, often on a daily basis. In addition to its own fast-growing national airline the Government of Qatar owns a 25 per cent stake in Gulf Air that operates an extensive regional and international schedule. As well as excellent passenger services, Doha International airport also offers first class cargo services.

Qatar Airways was founded in 1993 by a group of local prominent business executives. The airline has become one of the Emirate's most successful private companies. In 1997, the airline underwent a major re-launch with the help of a $19m loan from the

All of Qatar's trade, historically, was passed through its ports, and the modern fleet of tugs at Ras Laffan, (*above*) has a role to play in channelling the supertankers exporting LNG (Liquified Natural Gas).

The city of Doha is expanding fast, with a road network that is being constantly improved. The Al Gharrafa interchange *(below)* is the first three-level interchange on the peninsula.

Government. This re-launch encompassed the appointment of a new management team and a new corporate image including new uniforms for the staff and livery for the aircraft. Qatar Airways is one of the fastest growing airlines operating one of the youngest fleets in the world to 60 destinations in Europe, Middle East, Africa, Indian subcontinent and Asia. The airline, based in Doha, capital of the State of Qatar, operates a fleet of 39 modern all-Airbus aircraft. The airline is one of only three in the world to be awarded a Five Star ranking by Skytrax – the independent aviation industry monitoring agency – for high service standards and quality. As well as these services, Qatar Airways has code-sharing agreements with 100 other international airlines, greatly extending the range of destinations that it can offer.

Qatar's three ports offer world class facilities for handling all types of cargo, contributing to Qatar's role as a regional transport centre. Each

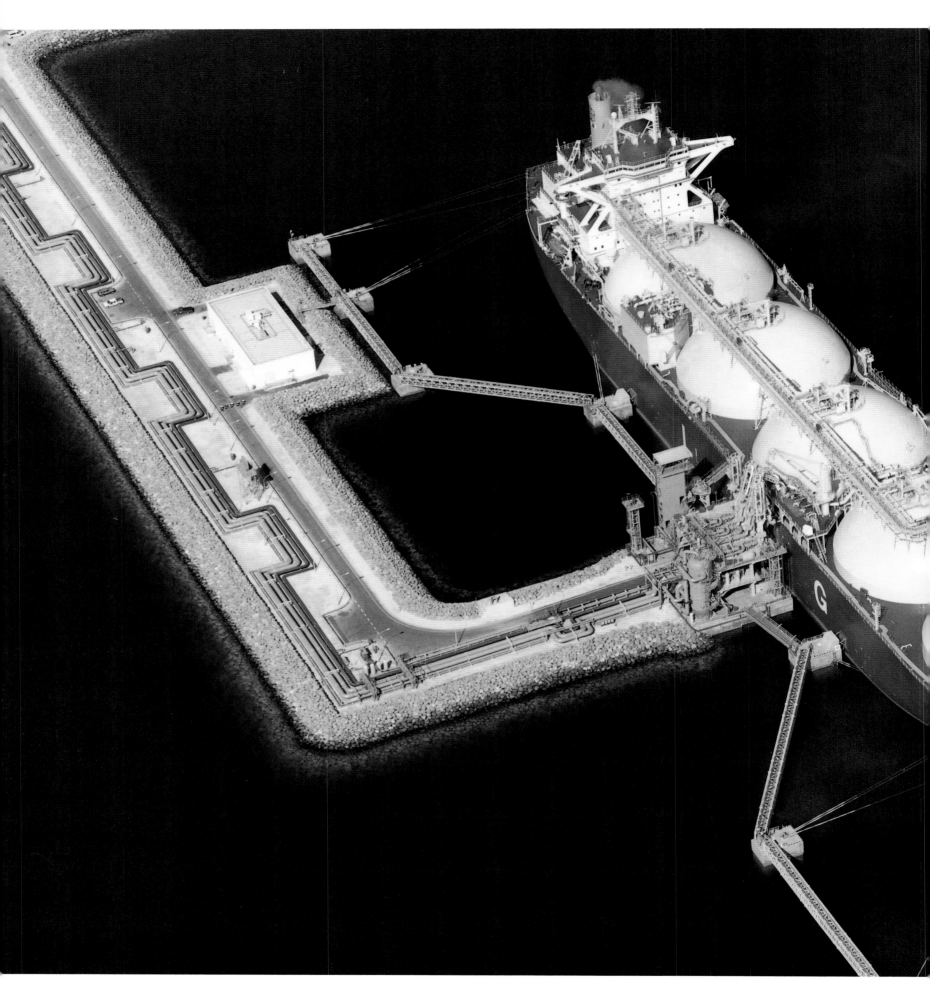

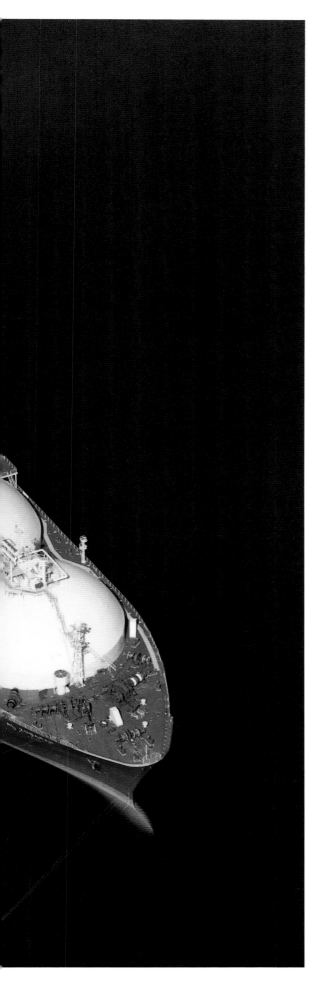

provides a specific service to companies involved in trading with Qatar. Doha port handles general cargo and containers, Messaieed handles oil exports and imports of oil-related equipment and at Ras Laffan Qatar possesses the world's largest and most modern liquified natural gas exporting facility.

**Doha's** port is located at the heart of the city, towards the southern end of the bay around which the city sits. The port plays a central role in Qatar's dynamic trading relations as it is the main entry and exit point for most general goods. It has Qatar's only container facility. The port has developed into today's top class facility from many centuries in the more humble role as a port for sail-powered *boums* trading the Gulf, as a fishing harbour and, later, as the centre for the country's pearl-fishing fleet.

**Messaieed** is Qatar's main oil export terminal and, thus, the terminus for the country's main oil and gas pipelines. In particular a pipeline links the port with the main oil field at Dukhan on Qatar's west coast. Messaieed's location on the country's east coast makes it ideally located for oil exports through the Straits of Hormuz to international oil markets. Almost all of Qatar's oil is exported through the port and it acts as the main entry point for imports of oil-related equipment. The availability of first class port facilities and easy access to fuel supplies has allowed Messaieed to support a wide range of industrial activities (see below, Manufacturing).

**Ras Laffan** port, located on Qatar's north-east coast, is the most modern of the country's port facilities and is part of the huge investment in the source of Qatar's future prosperity and development – gas. The port exclusively serves the huge liquefied natural gas (LNG) projects in Ras Laffan industrial city (see below). The largest LNG export facility in the world, the port covers an area of 8.5 sq.km. and is enclosed by two breakwaters – the main one 6 km in length and the lee breakwater 5.5 km long. Around 1.5 sq.km. of land was reclaimed as part of the port's construction, which began in 1992. The port was inaugurated in 1996. The port can accommodate two LNG vessels with a capacity of 135,000 cubic metres each, two liquid product vessels of 300,000 dead weight tonnes (dwt) and two dry cargo vessels of up to 20,000 dwt as well as exploration and production vessels up to 420m in length. As the country undertakes further development of its gas resources, the port's capacity will be increased.

The technology that makes LNG possible is highly sophisticated and transport of the 'miracle fuel' requires specialised ships, wharves and loading facilities.

The port at Ras Laffan (*below*) with its distinctive control tower (*right*) is the country's most modern and was purpose-built for LNG exports.

91

## Media

Since the early 1970s, Qatar has possessed television and radio stations that have served both Qataris with programmes in Arabic and the country's many foreign residents with programmes in English and other languages. In the mid-1990s, the range of services grew as Qatar took advantage of new methods of delivering television. Cable television networks were installed, offering a greater choice of viewing to Qatari audiences. This allowed Qatar to gain access to the global and regional satellite television channels that had gained in popularity. These facilities were further enhanced in 2002 with the advent of direct-to–satellite dishes for consumers.

## Al-Jazeera TV

Since its launch in November 1996, Al-Jazeera Television has made a marked impact on Arabic-language television, redefining the content and style of programming, especially in the area of current affairs and documentaries. The channel was established by a group of Qatari business executives supported by a government loan. The collapse of the BBC's Arabic-language satellite television earlier in the year provided a pool of talented journalists and production staff that the new station could exploit and combine with the excellent broadcasting facilities that already existed in the Emirate. Since late 1996, the satellite broadcasts of Al-Jazeera have grown rapidly in popularity throughout the Arab world. Its frank treatment of Middle Eastern political and cultural issues provides a refreshing alternative to the controlled output of many other regional and national television stations, and the channel's news and discussion programmes have broken new ground in Arabic-language television, introducing Middle Eastern audiences to a whole new diverse range of opinions.

## Telecommunications

A modern and rapidly growing economy requires a state-of-the-art and reliable telecommunications infrastructure. In these times of global businesses, executives rely on telecommunications to manage their companies and keep in contact with their clients, suppliers and advisers. Most business transactions from ordering goods to final payment require telecommunications. The infrastructure built by the Qatar Telecommunications company (Q-Tel) for business and domestic users now boasts over 350,000 telephone land lines, 100,000 mobile telephone lines and more than 10,000 internet subscribers. Mobile phones are compatible with the global standard for mobiles (GSM).This network provides modern communications throughout the country and integrates Qatar into the global communications system. Early in the twenty-first century, Qatar will have become directly connected to the fibre-optic cable linking Europe with Japan via the Gulf, known as FLAG. This cable will have become the backbone of worldwide communications and thus enhanced the Emirate's integration into the world telecommunications system.

The Government's continuing quest to

The information relayed from the productions suites of the Al-Jazeera newsroom is widely acclaimed as the most balanced and impartial news broadcast in the Arabic language (*opposite and left*).

Qatar Broadcasting Service – its headquarters pictured *below left* – covers the day's news with an interview on Doha's Corniche, *above*.

develop a modern economy in the country is encouraging the private sector to take a greater role in economic affairs and Q-Tel has been in the forefront of these efforts. It was one of the first companies to undergo privatisation in order to marry the strengths of the public and private sector to undertake future development of telecommunications. The fast pace of technological advance means that Q-Tel requires the maximum resources in order to maintain Qatar's leading edge in the provision of telecommunications services. In late 1998, the government launched the flotation of a 45 per cent stake in Q-Tel. Qatari and other Gulf investors were invited to purchase the shares, which were listed on the Doha Stock Market (DSM – see below). The sale raised $740m for

Q-Tel and was one of the first significant privatisations to occur in the Emirate. Its success set a precedent for future flotations.

### The Internet

Q-Tel is continually developing new telecommunications-related services and was the first Internet Service Provider (ISP) in the Emirate, providing Qatar's first gateway to the new economic opportunities created by the Internet and the worldwide web. As in the rest of the world, Internet use has grown rapidly in Qatar with Qatari companies and individuals taking advantage of the new medium. Most Qatari companies quickly developed sophisticated websites to establish their presence on the worldwide web and to spread word of their activities to a global audience. The government too has embraced the internet with e-Government, which provides a capability to check and process eleven different government services, from driving licence or health card renewal to visa applications and charitable donations.

## Oil & Gas

Qatar has proven, recoverable oil reserves of 15.2 billion barrels. In 2004, net oil exports totaled 1,023,000 barrels per day bpd. During this period, Qatar produced 1,068,000 bpd of liquids (including crude oil, natural gas liquids (NGLs), and condensate). Production of NGLs has been rising as a byproduct of increased natural gas production. The precise level of crude oil production and exports is determined by the prevailing OPEC quota, which exludes NGLs. The bulk of Qatar's reserves are found in the huge Dukhan oil field in the west of the peninsula. This contains around 2.2 billion barrels. The remaining is spread amongst Qatar's six offshore fields. All these fields contain oil with gravities in the 24-41º API range (the American Petroleum Institute Scale and  Scale) these produce two main types for export – Dukhan (41º API) and Marine (36º API).

## Qatar Petroleum (QP)

This is the umbrella company for all oil and gas activity in the Emirate. Founded as Qatar General Petroleum Corporation (QGPC) in July 1974 by Emiri decree, the company is responsible for exploration, drilling, production, maintenance and repair, transport, distribution, retail and the production of derivative products. The company has overall control of the industrial cities at Messaieed and Ras Laffan. It undertakes all these activities through a number of subsidiaries. QP's main subsidiaries include (extent of Qatari ownership in brackets):

National Oil Distribution Company
(NODCO – 100% QP)
Gulf Helicopter Company
(GHC – 100% QP)
Qatar Petrochemical Company
(QAPCO – 75% IQ)
Qatar Fertiliser Company
(QAFCO – 75% QP)
Ras Laffan LNG Company
(RasGas – 70% QP)
Qatar Liquefied Gas Company
(Qatargas – 65% QP)
Qatar Jet Fuel Company

Qatar's largest oil reserves are to be found in the Dukhan oil fields serviced by their own gas separating and processing plants.

QP (headquarters shown *right*) oversees all gas and oil activity in Qatar.

(QatarJet – 60% QP)
Qatar Chemical Company
(Q-Chem – 51% QP)
Qatar Fuel Additives Company
(QAFAC – 50% IQ)
Qatar Vinyl Company
(QVC – 25.5% QP, 31.9% QAPCO)
Qatar Shipping Company
(Q-Ship – 15% QP)
Qatar Electricity and Water Company
(QEWCO – 10% QP)

In addition, QP owns stakes in the following international operations (extent of stake in brackets):

Arab Shipbuilding and Repair Yard
(ASRY, Bahrain – 18.8%)
Arab Maritime Petroleum Transport Company
(AMPTC, Kuwait – 14.8%)
Arab Petroleum Investments Corporation
(APICORP, Saudi Arabia – 10%)
Arab Petroleum Services Company (APSC, Libya – 10%)
Arab Petroleum Pipelines Company (SUMED, Egypt – 5%)

Halul Island serves as the storage and export terminal for offshore oil.

## NODCO

The Natural Oil Distribution Company is solely responsible for the storage, refining, distribution and retail of oil and oil-related products in the Emirate. The company was founded for this purpose in 1968 and was absorbed as a wholly owned subsidiary by the newly formed QGPC in 1974. The company operates the pipelines that transport oil and gas around the country and to the export terminals. NODCO also operates the refinery at Messaieed. This is actually a combination of refineries. The first refinery was constructed here in 1953 and was replaced with a modern facility in 1974. A second refining unit was built adjacent to this facility in 1984 and as described below, further facilities have been added. The company's main products are butane, two grades of gasoline, kerosene, diesel and fuel oil. NODCO's subsidiary QatarJet in turn produces jet fuel.

## History of Exploration and Production

The discovery of oil provided Qatar with an economic lifeline and it is an inheritance that Qatar's rulers have used wisely. Although exploration for oil started in 1923, the first discoveries were not made until 1939 in what became known as the Dukhan field. This field remains the backbone of Qatar's oil production but has since been joined by at least six offshore

oil fields – the latest field to come on stream was the al-Karkara offshore field in 1998. Although production started almost immediately, due to the intervention of the Second World War Qatar had to wait another 10 years before the first exports of oil took place. The discovery and exploitation of oil occurred just as the pearl fishing industry was being extinguished by the introduction of cultivated pearls from Japan.

The oil industry has grown from modest beginnings to become the mainstay of the Qatari economy, a role now being taken over by gas.

In the early years of oil production, Dukhan, in the west of the peninsula, was Qatar's only producing field. In 1960, the first offshore fields were discovered. The first of these, Maydan Mahzam, came on-stream in 1965 and was joined in 1968 by the Idd al-Sharqi field. In 1973, the Bul Hanine offshore field started production. In the 1990s, al-Rayyan, al-Shaheen and al-Khalij as well as al-Karkara joined these offshore fields. Meanwhile exploration for new fields both onshore and offshore continues, as does development work at existing fields. Projects to boost production at Bul Hanine and at Idd al-Sharqi are underway. Advanced technology means that the operational lifespan of Qatar's fields can be greatly extended. Although the Emirate has placed a great emphasis on the development of its gas resources, the effective

management and development of its oil resources remains a top priority. Oil remains an important international commodity and Qatar maintains ample resources to help satisfy demand for oil.

The revenues from oil have allowed Qatar to develop the modern and sophisticated economy that it enjoys, and revenues from oil exports will remain an important contributor to financing the country's economic development. During the earliest years of oil production, Qatar received only modest revenues from oil production, mainly in the form of fees paid by companies for the right to explore and produce oil as well as a percentage of profits from the sale of oil, but these revenues were almost immediately put to use for Qatar's economic and social well-being. Within the first decade of oil exports, the process of industrial development was launched with the construction of the first refinery at Messaieed. In the same time period, the first schools and hospitals were built. Qatar's development, financed with oil revenues, made steady progress in the 1960s, but the real advances came after the sharp price increases in 1973 imposed by OPEC and the negotiation of new structures with the oil companies. Qatar had been a member of the organisation since 1961. In 1974, the Government gained more effective control over oil-related activities with the creation of the Qatar General Petroleum Company (QGPC)

The NODCO refineries based in Messaieed in the south receive fuel piped from the north and turn it into various grades of gasoline, kerosene, diesel and lubricating oil.

Natural gas sourced from Qatar's immense North Field is increasingly seen as the fuel of the future *(opposite)*.

renamed as Qatar Petroleum (QP), which has responsibility for all oil-related activities in the Emirate, either directly or through its subsidiaries and joint ventures. The company has also played a key role in developing other industrial activities.

## Downstream Development

Qatar's first refinery was constructed at Messaieed in 1953, some four years after the first oil exports. From this small start, Qatar has constructed the modern distribution, refining and petrochemical industries that now exist in the country and allow it to take full advantage of its oil resources. NODCO, a subsidiary of QP oversees all downstream oil activity. NODCO operates the refinery at Messaieed, distributes oil to domestic customers and to export terminals as well as being responsible for the retail of oil and oil products in Qatar. In 1999, NODCO completed the upgrade of the Messaieed refinery. This increased its capacity from just less than 57,000 barrels per day (bpd) to around 83,000 bpd. The project also included the construction

of a unit to refine condensate, with a capacity of 30,000 bpd. A further condensate refining unit is planned to bring the refinery's eventual capacity up to 137,000 bpd.

## Future Developments

The increase in oil production since 1995 is the result of a deliberate government policy to reinvigorate the country's oil industry and ensures that it remains a dynamic contributor to the Emirate's economic success. In order to achieve this reinvigoration and to ensure the future prosperity of the industry, QP has brought in foreign partners for their expertise and resources. The exploitation of new offshore fields at Al-Rayyan, al-Khalij, al-Shaheen and al-Karkara have added production capacity. The foreign partners in these projects have included major oil companies such as Arco, Elf Aquitaine, Agip, Maersk and Occidental Petroleum. The companies are undertaking these projects under the terms of production sharing agreements, which are typically of 25 years' length. These projects represent the future operating method for the industry – combining the best of the public and private sector interests.

Qatar is determined not to rest on its laurels and to continue searching for new oil resources. In March 1998, the QP signed a five-year agreement with the US oil company Chevron for it to conduct onshore exploration. The agreement covers exploration over virtually the remainder of the peninsula outside the Dukhan field. This amounts to some 4,200 square miles of territory. Chevron also holds the rights to exploration of an offshore block.

### Natural Gas

Qatar has been blessed with huge reserves of the fuel for the twenty-first century – natural gas. Natural gas is esteemed for its after-burn cleanliness, and the volume of energy per cubic unit in the liquefied form.

Qatar has the third largest reserves in the world and possesses the largest non-associated gas field in the world, North Field. Although a great deal of emphasis is naturally placed on the North Field, it is not Qatar's sole source of gas. Many of Qatar's oil fields contain associated gas fields and these form an important part of Qatar's gas resources. They are an important source for condensates and natural gas. Natural gas is increasingly popular as a fuel due to its wide availability and its impact on the environment. The consumption of natural gas is less damaging to the environment than the burning of oil or coal, and in these environmentally aware times, this is a significant bonus. Natural gas can be used as a fuel for power generation, industrial processes and for domestic purposes. In addition, natural gas can be used as a feedstock, or primary raw ingredient, in the petrochemical industry. Overall, natural gas is a versatile and clean commodity.

The existence of natural gas in large quantities beneath Qatar's territorial waters has been known for some time. The North Field was discovered in 1971. However, the commercial exploitation of natural gas started only in the 1980s though due to changes in economic and technological conditions. Several factors combined to make the exploitation of natural gas a more attractive proposition. The successful production and consumption of natural gas takes considerable investment and for many years was viewed as commercially unfeasible. These factors included greater uncertainty over global oil prices, a higher level of environmental awareness and the development of suitable technology.

The uncertainty over oil prices and the desire to diversify the economy led the Qatari government to develop other economic activities. Using Qatar's other substantial natural resource – gas – seemed an obvious choice, especially as the demand for this increasingly popular fuel was rising. The development of suitable technology to allow gas producers to drill for and process natural gas into a form that can be more easily transported created the conditions for the commercially feasible exploitation of the country's natural gas resources.

The development of technology that allows the transportation of natural gas over long distances without the need for the construction of pipelines has allowed Qatar to satisfy demand for gas in distant markets. Qatar's main customers for natural gas are the economies of East Asia, particularly Japan and South Korea. When LNG exports to these countries started in 1996, their economies were booming as the Asian 'tigers' reached their economic peak. The Asian financial crisis of 1997 threatened to dampen the demand for gas (and for oil) but these countries continued to need to import most of their energy needs.

In order to diversify its customer base, the Qatari LNG exporters have signed supply agreements with India and other new customers are also being sought.

Immense refineries, such as the QAPCO facility in Messaieed shown here, take the raw resources piped from the North Field and turn them into usable end products.

There is plenty of scope for the development of LNG exports as worldwide demand for gas is rising and Qatar has the infrastructure in place to meet that demand. Countries such as the USA will find it increasingly difficult to meet its natural gas requirements from their own resources. The need to cut carbon emissions into the atmosphere as part of international agreements is contributing to the increased demand for natural gas throughout the developed world. Although there are other countries in the world that have substantial natural gas resources such as Russia and Iran as well as Central Asian states such as Turkmenistan, the LNG production and export infrastructure in these states is not as well developed as in Qatar.

### The North Field

The basis for Qatar's huge potential as a provider of gas lies with the North Field, located, as its name suggests, off the north shore of the peninsula. The field was discovered in 1971 and has proven to be the world's largest

Qatar Gas brings together both public and private sector investment to build the vast offshore infrastructure required for gas extraction (*above*), and also runs the extensive onshore facilities (*below*).

non-associated gas field (i.e. it is not part of a structure that also contains oil). The field has proven recoverable reserves of at least 380 trillion cubic feet (tcf) and its total reserves are estimated at more than 500 tcf. The field covers more than 6,000 sq. km., equivalent to almost half of Qatar's land area.

The upstream exploitation of North Field gas is undertaken under a development and production sharing agreement. This agreement is a joint venture between QP and the following international companies – Total, ExxonMobil, Mitsui and MQL. QP has a 65 per cent stake in this joint venture, Total 20 per cent, ExxonMobil 10 per cent, Mitsui and MQL 2.5 per cent each. Exploitation of this huge resource started in 1987 with the launch of Phase 1 designed to produce gas for domestic use and a limited amount for export. Phase 2, the production of significant amounts of gas for export, got underway in 1997 with the first major exports from the Qatargas project. The focus for activities associated with the exploitation of the North Field's resources is the industrial city of Ras Laffan, located on Qatar's north-eastern shore on the southern edge of the field. The city is purpose - built to serve the gas industry.

### The LNG Process

Although in many ways gas is an ideal fuel, several challenges have to be met before it can be successfully used. For Qatar, one of the main challenges is its distance from potential markets in Asia. Gas, in its raw state, is a difficult substance to transport over long distances due to its inflammability and bulk. Unlike crude oil, gas cannot simply be loaded onto a ship and transported to market. The solution to the transportation challenge lies in liquefaction. A barrel of liquefied gas is the equivalent of 600 barrels of 'gaseous' gas. Liquefied, gas is far less bulky to transport. Liquefying requires the construction of specialised facilities close to the gas field and the construction of facilities in the final market to re-gassify the gas so that it can be used as fuel. These facilities represent significant investments and therefore producers such as Qatar have to confirm long-term contracts in order to justify the construction of such facilities. Consumer countries such as Japan and South Korea must also have confidence in the long-term security of supply from gas-producing states.

After gas is extracted from the North Field, it is piped ashore to Ras Laffan. The crude natural gas that comes ashore is a mixture of chemicals, including gases such as propane and butane as well as liquids. These liquids are known as condensates as they are gases that have condensed under the pressure of the gas field. The first stage in the liquefaction process is the

separation of these condensates from the gases. In the next stage, impurities such as water, carbon dioxide and mercury are removed from the mixture. High quality gases are then separated from the remainder. These gases are then compressed and refrigerated using liquid nitrogen to achieve the very low temperatures needed to turn the gas into liquid. The result is liquefied natural gas (LNG). The equipment used in the preparation of LNG is often referred to as a 'train' as it is a series of units linked together, like the carriages of a train. An LNG plant will often consist of more than one 'train' and the capacity of each 'train' is usually given in tonnes per annum i.e. the amount of LNG capable of being produced in a year. The LNG is then stored at temperatures of around −160ºC before being loaded onto LNG carrier ships for transport to market. At its destination, the LNG is then returned to gaseous form before being distributed to consumers such as industry and power generators.

**The Qatar Liquefied Gas Company (Qatargas)**
Qatargas was the first company established to take advantage of the immense opportunities that flow from Qatar's possession of extensive gas reserves. In many ways, the company has demonstrated the way forward for other Qatari companies. As well as utilising the latest technology to exploit the fuel of the future – gas

The LNG process is highly complex and necessitates the piping of nitrogen gas in liquid form to assist in reaching the incredibly low temperatures required for natural gas compression and liquefication. Parts of this process are shown here at the LNG plant in Messaieed.

– it brings together private and public sector allowing Qatari and foreign companies to maximise resources and expertise. The shareholders and the extent of their holding are as follows:

|  | Upstream | Downstream |
|---|---|---|
| QP | 65% | 65% |
| Total | 20% | 10% |
| ExxonMobil Qatar | 10% | 10% |
| Mitsui | 2.5% | 7.5% |
| Marubeni | 2.5% | 7.5% |

The company was established in 1984 and its primary commercial activity is the operation of an LNG plant at Ras Laffan and export of the product. This plant consists of three 'trains' each with a capacity of 2 million metric tonnes per annum (MMTA). The last of these was completed in 1999, bringing the project up to full capacity. Expansions will bring the level to 9.5 MMTA at the end of 2005. The addition of two more trains by 2010 will double that capacity. The LNG produced at this plant is exported to customers in Japan. The LNG production process also results in some useful by-products export. These include condensates and sulphur – both of which Qatargas exports from Ras Laffan port.

The facilities operated by Qatargas also include offshore plants and support services for these production facilities and the staff that operate them. The offshore facilities consist of wellhead platforms, a central processing unit and an accommodation platform for the staff operating the offshore facilities. The central process unit provides some processing of the gas before it is sent onshore for liquefaction. The onshore facilities include the three-train LNG plant, storage and loading facilities and a wide range of support services. These include power generation, water supply, medical and safety and security services. Qatargas also provides accommodation and social clubs for its staff on its own compound.

Qatargas is also responsible for the transport of the LNG to its Japanese customers. It does this through its subsidiary Qatargas Commercial and Shipping (QCS). The company has a fleet of ten carriers, each with a capacity of 135,000 cubic metres. Each carrier is named after a city, town or

The immense tanks shown here store the LNG at high pressures prior to being loaded onto the LNG tankers on the jetty alongside.

area in Qatar – al-Zubarah, al-Khor, al-Rayyan, al-Wajbah, Broog, al-Wakrah, Doha, Zekreet, al-Bidda and al-Jasra. The ships have a cruising speed of 20 knots and the round trip to Japan takes approximately one month. Major contracts were signed in 2005 to vastly expand the fleet.

## RasGas

RasGas Company Limited was established in 2001 by QP (70%) and ExxonMobil (30%), to assume responsibility for providing a full range of operations and maintenance management services to the first development Ras Laffan Liquefied Natural Gas Company Limited, established in 1993 with a production capacity of 6.6 MMTA; Ras Laffan Liquefied Natural Gas Company Limited II, established in 2001 adding two trains to provide an additional 9.56 MMTA; the Al Khaleej Gas Project (AKG) and future expansion opportunities. The company commenced operations in July 2002.

Future projects include RasGas LNG train 5 (4.7 MMTA), large LNG trains 6 and 7 (7.8 MMTA each), and additional AKG pipeline gas sales capacity. RasGas' major customers are Korea Gas Corporation (KOGAS), Petronet PLL of India, Edison Gas of Italy as well as ExxonMobil, British Gas LNG, LG Caltex, Emirates National Oil Co. (ENOC), Idemitsu Kosan-Japan, SK Energy and CMS.

## The Dolphin Project

Dolphin Energy Limited was created to develop substantial energy projects throughout the Gulf Co-operation Council (GCC). Its objective is to create long-term economic wealth and new business opportunities for GCC citizens, far into the future.

Dolphin Energy's major strategic initiative, the Dolphin Project, involves the production and processing of natural gas from Qatar's North Field, and transportation of the dry gas by pipeline to the UAE, beginning in 2006.

The Foundation Stone for Dolphin Energy's Gas Processing Plant in Qatar was formally laid on 29 May 2005 in Ras Laffan Industrial City. The $1.6 billion Gas Processing Plant will process raw gas from Qatar's North Field – removing valuable by-products such as condensates and Liquified Petroleum Gas (LPG)for international sale. The resulting refined gas will then flow over 370 kilometers through Dolphin's dedicated Export Pipeline to Abu Dhabi, for distribution to customers throughout the UAE.

Dolphin Energy's first initiative, the Al Ain to Fujairah Pipeline, came on stream in January 2004.The pipeline supplies the Fujairah Water and Power Plant on the UAE's East Coast – initially with natural gas from Oman, and subsequently with Dolphin gas from Qatar.

Dolphin Energy is owned 51 per cent by Mubadala Development Company, on behalf of the Government of Abu Dhabi – and 24.5 percent each by Total of France and Occidental Petroleum of the USA.

Supplies are brought by helicopter to the North Field installation (*above and left*).

## Petrochemicals

Qatar's extensive oil and gas resources have allowed the Emirate to develop a strong petrochemical industry that now makes a substantial contribution to the country's economy. The development of petrochemicals is a natural progression as the Qatari economy becomes more sophisticated and moves towards the production of high value-added products. The origins of Qatar's petrochemical industry can be traced back to the construction of the first refinery in 1953. Refining crude oil is the most basic of petrochemical activities. The petrochemical industry really took off after 1974 when the Qatar Petrochemical Company (QAPCO, see below) was established. Since those early days, Qatar has established a wide range of petrochemical companies to produce chemicals from oil and gas feedstocks.

These petrochemical projects combine Qatar's huge natural resources with modern technology and outside expertise to create industrial enterprises. As a result they add to the diversification of the Qatari economy and extend the range of the Emirate's exports. Bringing together the country's natural resources with modern technology also allows Qatari nationals to acquire new skills and expertise. These projects, in turn, produce chemicals that can be used as raw products in other manufacturing enterprises.

The main centre for the petrochemical industry is the city of Messaieed. The city provides excellent infrastructure for industrial enterprises with easy access to fuel and feedstock sources and the port for the export of goods and import of essential supplies. The city is also close to the capital, Doha, for easy access to the Government, financial centre and the international airport. Messaieed will remain the main focus for the industry, but other cities will also develop petrochemical facilities. There are plans for petrochemical facilities in Ras Laffan, alongside the LNG plants, to take advantage of the easy access to natural gas as a fuel and feedstock. Many petrochemical processes use natural gas (or gases derived from it) rather than oil-based chemicals as feedstock.

### Qatar Vinyl Company (QVC)

QVC is one of Qatar's most modern enterprises and represents the developing nature of Qatar's industrial capability. QVC will use the output of Qatar's petrochemical industries to manufacture products for export and for use by other Qatari companies. QVC's operations will also encourage the creation of other companies to supply essential materials. The company was formed by Emiri decree in December 1997 following the signing of a joint venture agreement between Qatari and foreign companies. The company's shareholders are:

QP – 25.5%
QAPCO – 31.9%
Norsk Hydro – 29.7%
Elf Atochem – 12.9%

An analyst studies product quality specifications in one of QAPCO's product development labs.

Ethylene, a product of the petrochemical industry, produced at QAPCO's Massaieed plant is an intermediate in the manufacture of other chemicals such as polythene and plastics *(above)*.

Construction of the company's facilities at Messaieed got underway in early 1999 after the signing of an agreement with a German-Italian consortium. The plant is scheduled for commissioning in 2001 and will produce ethylene dichloride, vinyl chloride monomer and caustic soda. The first two chemicals are widely used as raw materials in the plastics industry. QAPCO provides the ethylene feedstock and purchases around 28 per cent of the company's output. The remainder is intended for export with East Asian countries forming the most significant markets.

## Qatar Salt Company

The QVC project will also require salt as one of its essential inputs and there are plans to develop a salt processing capability in Qatar. The salt project would use the waste material from the Emirate's two desalination plants and seawater to produce salt. The main emphasis of the project would be the production of salt for industrial use, such as in the QVC plant but also for export. The plant would also produce salt suitable for human consumption for use in food and for retail. The salt project is the brainchild of Qatari and German investors.

## Qatar Industrial Manufacturing Company (QIMCO)

The Government is determined to encourage private sector involvement in the economy and

QIMCO represents the tangible expression of this policy. Established in 1990 with a capital of QR200 million, QIMCO aims to set up ventures in various fields of industrial production at home and in the GCC countries, develop its marketing and commercial capabilities and help subsidiary companies to secure a reasonable share of the market. In 1999, the company's direct investment reached QR320 million in more than 16 industrial projects. QR143 million of this capital is paid by the company while the balance is covered by financial facilities from commercial banks.

Among the investments are;
Qatar Clay Bricks Company
Qatar Metal Coating Company
Qatar Jet Fuel Company
National Paper Industries Company
Gulf Ferro Alloys Company
Qatar Sand Treatment Plant
National Chemical Industries Company
Qatari-Saudi Gypsum Industry Company
National Food Company.

QIMCO's development of Qatar's manufacturing capability integrates different aspects of Qatari industry. Its projects are set to enhance Qatar's ability to become self sufficient in some products and to reduce the country's reliance on imports. Some examples are:

**Qatar Plastic Products Company** – a joint venture between QIMCO, QAPCO and the

Italian company Febo, with each company enjoying an approximate third share and represents an investment of US$40 million. The company manufactures heavy duty plastic bags using chemicals supplied by QAPCO, which in turn will use the bags for packaging its products. At peak production the company will manufacture 22 million plastic bags per year.

**Qatar Hot Briquetted Iron Company (QABISCO)** – is an iron works at Messaieed with production at 2 million tonnes per year. The project represents a total investment of QR1.5 billion in a joint venture between QIMCO (45 per cent), QASCO (34.5 per cent), Qatar Shipping Company (11 per cent) and private sector investors (10 per cent).

**Qatar Nitrogen Company** – this is a joint venture between QIMCO and QP with each holding a 50 per cent stake. When fully operational, the company's plant in Messaieed will produce both gaseous and liquid nitrogen. The latter is an essential requirement in the LNG process and therefore the company will make an important contribution to the country's economic development.

**Qatar Petrochemical Company (QAPCO)**
QAPCO is the oldest of Qatar's petrochemical companies but has invested in modern technology and management methods to ensure that it remains at the cutting edge. When the company

was formed in 1974, it was a pioneer company in more ways than one. As well as being the Emirate's first petrochemical company, it was one of the first to involve a joint venture between the public and foreign private sectors. The company is a joint venture between the QP (holding 80 per cent), the French company Elf Atochem (10 per cent) and the Italian company Enichem (10 per cent). The company's plant and offices are located in Messaieed, where it employs around 830 people in a 24-hour operation. The plant receives natural gas as a feedstock from Dukhan in the west and the North Field. These facilities are used to produce ethylene, low density polyethylene and sulphur, all chemicals used as raw materials for other manufacturing plants in the country and for export. The main markets for QAPCO's products are other Middle Eastern states, India, Pakistan and Australia with around 45 per cent of its total production going for export.

### Qatar Fuel Additives Company (QAFAC)

QAFAC is one of the most modern petrochemical facilities in the country. Its plant at Messaieed was inaugurated in October 1999 by the Emir of Qatar. The company was first formed in 1990 as joint venture involving QP (50 per cent), the Chinese Petroleum Company (20 per cent), Lee Chang Yung Chemical Industry Corporation (15 per cent) and International Octane Limited (15 per cent). Construction on the plant started in 1997 and when it is fully operational it is intended to produce 825,000 metric tonnes of methanol and 610,000 tonnes of Methyl Tertiary-Butyl Ether per year. Both chemicals are added to gasoline to produce cleaner-burning fuel for automobiles. QAFAC's products are intended for export. The plant will undergo continued investment in modern technology to take into account stricter environmental controls taking effect around the world.

Fertilisers produced here at the plant in Messaieed (*above*) are another by-product of the oil industry.

### Qatar Steel Company (QASCO)

Aside from the production of crude oil, QASCO represents the oldest heavy industry enterprise in the country. The company was formed in 1975 as a joint venture between the Qatari Government and two Japanese companies – Kobe Steel and Tokyo Boeki with the Government holding 70 per cent of the company. The company's plant was completed in 1978 at Messaieed. In 1997, the company undertook a major strategic review and put in place a 10 year investment programme. One of the first actions was the Government's buyout of the remaining 30 per cent stake from Kobe Steel

and Tokyo Boeki. The programme calls for $1.75 billion investment in the ten-year period to increase both the volume of production and the range of products. This would allow QASCO to use the latest technology to develop a range of high-value added products.

### Qatar Chemical Company (Q-Chem)

Q-Chem exemplifies the continued development of Qatar's petrochemical industry in combination with foreign partners. Q-Chem is one of Qatar's newest large companies. The company was formed in 1997 when a joint

venture agreement was signed between QP and the US company Phillips Petroleum. In 1999, Q-Chem signed an agreement with the international company Kellogg Brown and Root (KBR) for the engineering, procurement and construction of its plant. KBR was also committed to providing the technology for the manufacturing process. The plant was expected to produce half a million tonnes per year of ethylene, low density and high density polyethylene as well as 47,000 tonnes of hexene-1. The construction project was expected to employ 5,000 people at its peak and was scheduled for completion in 2001. Full production is expected to get underway the following year.

## Qatar Fertiliser Company (QAFCO)

QAFCO was the first company formed in Qatar to take advantage of the country's potential for petrochemicals. QAFCO was formed in 1969 and its plant was the first to be constructed at the then newly formed industrial city of Messaieed. The plant was completed in 1973 and produces ammonia and urea. In 1974, the company was brought under the umbrella of QP as a joint venture with QP holding 75 per cent and the Norwegian company Norsk Hydro holding the remainder. The company has grown into one of the world's major producers of fertiliser products. In 1974, production stood at 120,000 tonnes of ammonia and 70,000 tonnes of urea but by 1999, this had grown to 1.3 and 1.6 million tonnes respectively. QAFCO has expanded in three distinct phases, following the completion of the initial establishment in 1974, the plant was expanded in 1979 and the third phase was completed in 1997. The fourth phase of expansion was completed in 2003 and made QAFCO the largest producer of ammonia and urea in the world. The company's efforts to minimise the environmental impact of its activities were recognised in 1997 when it received The International Standardisation Award 14001. The company has also gained ISO 9002 certification.

## Qatar Lubricants Company (QALCO)

QALCO is the first enterprise in Qatar geared towards producing lubricants. The company was founded in 1997 and is primarily geared towards meeting demand in the Qatari market. The company has production facilities for 20,000 tonnes of lubricants as well as laboratories to develop new products. The company is a subsidiary of Qatar Industrial Services Company.

## Gas to Liquids

Taking full advantage of exciting new technologies, Qatar Petroleum is actively pursuing a number of world-scale gas-to-liquids conversion projects for the production of synthetic fuels and base oil stocks. The projects are all integrated with offshore development to supply the large amounts of gas needed for these projects. These are active business opportunities that are being pursued, but the status of each of the projects is still in the early stages.

Among the downstream products of Qatar's hydro-carbons is urea (*right*), exported on a large scale for plastics and fertiliser.

### Oryx GTL Project

All major project agreements have been signed with the relevant parties. Oryx GTL Ltd. was established at the end of January 2003 as a joint venture company between Qatar Petroleum (51%) and Sasol (49%). The GTL plant will be ready for start-up in December 2005 and first product will enter the international market during the second quarter of 2006.

### Sasol Chevron

Sasol Chevron submitted a Project Profile Proposal to QP in July 2002 for an integrated upstream/downstream GTL project to produce 120,000 bpd of GTL product in two phases. The project will produce naphtha and diesel as the primary products. A Statement of Intent was signed for this project in November 2002. Initial indications were for

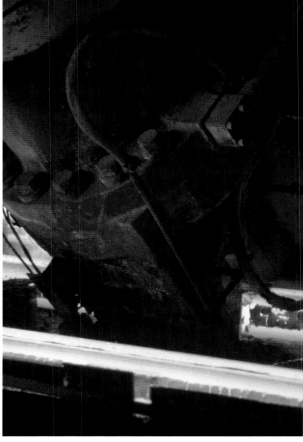

The ready availability of cheap fuel makes Qatar a logical site for steel production - a process with a high energy requirement. The export of Qatari steel continues to play an important role in the country's economy (*above, right and far right*).

### Pearl GTL

Shell's GTL is an integrated project which will develop about 1.6 billion cubic feet per day of North Field gas to produce approximately 140,000 bpd of synthetic fuels and base oils. The project will be developed in two phases with the first phase operational in 2009, producing around 70,000 bpd of GTL products with the second phase to be completed less than two years later. Qatar Petroleum and Qatar Shell GTL Limited (Shell) signed the Development and Production Sharing Agreement (DPSA) for Pearl GTL in July 2004.

startup of the project by 2010, but a revised startup date will be produced when the next round of negotiations with Sasol Chevron commences.

### ExxonMobil

ExxonMobil GTL project is for the production of synthetic GTL products in excess of 150,000 bpd. Feedstock for the GTL Plant will be provided from two wellhead platforms; approximately 1.8 billion cubic feet per day will be required to yield the target GTL production. The project will produce base oil stocks in addition to the synthetic fuels. The HOA signed in July 2004 specifies the principal terms for the project that will be defined in a Development and Production Sharing Agreement (DPSA). The term of the DPSA will be 25 years from the start of production, which is expected to commence in 2011.

## Marathon

The Marathon GTL project will produce approximately 120,000 bpd of naphtha and

the GTL plant. Startup of the first phase of the plant is scheduled for 2010. The project is structured on the basis of a Production Sharing Agreement, as with all other large-scale GTL projects.

## Industries Qatar (IQ)

In a move to partially privatise state-owned industries, Industries Qatar was formed in April

diesel. The project will consist of two trains of equal capacity. Phase I first commercial production is planned for 2010. Offshore development is based on two unmanned wellhead platforms and two wet scheme pipelines configuration.

## ConocoPhillips

ConocoPhillips is planning to develop its GTL project in two phases, each producing approximately 80,000 bpd of GTL products - naphtha and diesel using CoPOX technology. Two wellhead platforms with adequate number of wells will provide the required feedstock for

2003, to take over the interests held by the government in four Messaieed industrial companies. Industries of Qatar is listed on the Doha Securities Market (DSM) and had an initial public offering (IPO) covering 15 per cent of its authorised share capital of QR 5,000 million ($1,370 million).

QP transferred all its controlling shares in Qatar Fertiliser Company (QAFCO), Qatar Petrochemical Company (QAPCO) and Qatar Fuel Additives Company (QAFAC) to the new company, in addition to the state share in Qatar Steel Company (QASCO). The IPO was the largest since the government sell-off of a 45 per

Traditionally a seafaring nation, Qatar relies heavily to this day on ships for the bulk of its export.

By-products from the oil industry are numerous and form a separate set of export businesses aside from Qatar's core energy production.

The Telecommunications building *(opposite, right)* is an example of innovative modern architecture and construction in Doha.

cent stake in Qatar Telecom (Q-Tel) and is part of a strategy to give the private sector a greater economic role.

## Manufacturing

Economic diversification is one of the Government's prime economic policies and one that it has pursued with vigour. The development of manufacturing capabilities beyond the petrochemical sector is an important part of this diversification process. Although the Government has played a key role in stimulating the creation of manufacturing industries, it has also encouraged the private sector to play its full role. The result of these forward-looking economic policies is a diverse range of manufacturing companies in Qatar including plastics, paper, chemicals and construction materials. Much of this manufacturing capacity has developed since 1973, when Qatar gained the full benefit from its oil resources but the origins of manufacturing lie before this. Manufacturing of a limited kind has probably always occurred on the peninsula

since it has been inhabited. For much of the peninsula's history this probably consisted of no more than small craft workshops and traditional boat-building enterprises using imported materials. The first modern manufacturing facility was established in 1965, when a cement factory was founded at Umm Bab on Qatar's western coast. Production at the factory did not actually start until 1969. After 1973, there was an explosion of manufacturing enterprises, commencing with the establishment of the Qatar Steel Company in 1975. These ventures continue to flourish and formulate plans for expansion, while new ventures are put into effect.

## Construction

The construction sector has become one of the most dynamic in the Qatari economy as the demand for new facilities, infrastructure and buildings rises. Throughout most of the 1990s, Qatar was able to commence two to three major projects annually. This represented a major impetus for the success of the sector. During the early part of the twenty-first

century that rate increased dramatically spurred on by vast new wealth from the oil and more importantly gas industries and the need for a very modern infrastructure to accommodate the Asian Games in 2006. In addition, Qatar's developing role as a regional and international commercial centre creates demand for the construction of new facilities. In 2000 Doha was anticipating a boom in construction of hotels and conference facilities. These are required to cater for the expected rise in business visitors, as Doha becomes a popular destination for major business conferences and exhibitions.

## Major Projects

A series of major infrastructure projects were seen as dominating the construction sector between 2000 and 2010. These projects would include:

**Ras Laffan Integrated Water and Power Plant** (IWPP) was one of the most exciting projects in Qatar, since it marked a new stage in the development of the Emirate's infrastructure.

The plant is the first such integrated facility constructed in Qatar and as its name suggests it provides water and electricity for the Ras Laffan Industrial City. The company is a joint venture between AES of America (50%), Qatar Electricity and Water Company (30%), QP (10%) and Gulf Investment Company (10%). The cost of the plant was QR2.55 billion with a capacity to produce 750MW of electricity and 40 million gallons per day of desalinated water. Electrical production started in 2003 and water in 2004.

Dolphin, as already noted, is one of the largest energy projects ever conceived and foresees $8-10 billion investment over six to seven years. An essential element of the project is the construction of a pipeline from the North Field to Abu Dhabi and on to Dubai and Oman (and possibly eventually to Pakistan).

The New Doha International Airport will position Doha and Qatar as a leading regional aviation hub and it will be pivotal to the continued growth of Qatar Airways — the national airline.

The new green-field airport will be situated four kilometers east of the existing airport. It will comprise two runways partially constructed on reclaimed land, a 24-gate passenger terminal complex capable of handling 12 million passengers a year, a new Amiri (Royal) Terminal with additional hardstands, a cargo terminal building, aircraft hangars, and associated airline and airport ancillary features, including 25,000 square meters devoted to retail space.

Scheduled for full completion in 2015, construction of the new state-of-the-art airport will take place in three phases. Phase one, due to commence next year, will cost more than $2 billion and will include reclaiming nearly half of the site from the sea with 50 million cubic metres of fill, a 140,000-square-metre, three-storey terminal with 24 contact gates, and three road interchanges to access the new airport. Detailed design work will continue throughout 2004 and 2005 as the site is reclaimed and construction of the new major facilities will begin from 2005.

## Banking and Finance

As befits a modern and dynamic economy, Qatar possesses a sophisticated and well-regulated banking system. Qatari banks have a strong capital base, offer a wide range of services to corporate and personal customers and operate under the regulation of the Qatar Central Bank (QCB). The QCB now oversees a booming banking sector that consists of 14 commercial institutions including Qatari, foreign and Islamic banks and one specialised institution – Qatar Industrial Development Bank. The QCB was created in 1993, when it replaced the Qatar Monetary Agency, which was formed in 1973 in the early days of Qatari independence. At the same time, the Qatari Riyal was introduced as the national currency. This agency replaced an earlier currency board established in the 1960s.

In 1966, the Qatar-Dubai Riyal was introduced as currency to replace the Indian rupee that had previously circulated as currency. The modern Qatari Riyal has proven a stable and reliable currency.

The banking sector in Qatar is dominated by four institutions – Qatar National Bank, Doha Bank, Commercial Bank of Qatar and al-Ahli Bank. It has shown strong growth. In 1998, profits rose by more than 25 per cent, continuing the trend of strong growth throughout much of the 1990s. The prospects for the sector look good as banks benefit from liberalisation measures introduced in the mid and late 1990s. In 1995, some restrictions on interest rates were relaxed. In 1998, almost all controls on interest rates were lifted. In

addition, the QCB introduced treasury bills and bonds, which were offered for sale to Qatari banks. The move was part of re-evaluation of the Government's monetary policy and the introduction of a more active policy on the part of the QCB. This policy should ensure that Qatar's economy and financial system retain the stability that they have long enjoyed and which has allowed business to flourish.

Qatar Financial Centre was launched in May 2005, a hub for internatonal finance companies to operate under highly favourable terms similar to an "off-shore" set-up. This includes the creation of a new legal framework governing the business run from the QFC, and separate from the state laws of Qatar, low rent, and favourable tax breaks. The QFC is presented as a chance for world-class companies to set up office and share in the vibrant financial industry related to the oil and gas boom.

**Stock Market**

The establishment of the Doha Securities Market (DSM) in May 1997 marked a significant step forward in the development and expansion of financial services in the Emirate. The DSM provides exciting new investment opportunities in the Emirate and creates a new channel for Qatari companies to raise finance for expansion plans and new projects. The 35 per cent rise in the DSM index in 1998 (its first full year of operation) demonstrates the appetite for investment in stocks and shares amongst Qataris. This increase made the DSM the best-performing stock exchange in the Arab world. Until early 2000, only Qatari nationals were permitted to invest in the DSM. This was extended to all Gulf Co-operation Council (GCC) nationals with cabinet approval in February 2000. The market was further opened

The city of Doha has sprung up and sprawled out from the wide smooth sweep of the sculptured Corniche *(below, and opposite top and bottom)* and continues to grow outwards into the surrounding desert. The growth, fuelled by oil and gas wealth, has led to a thriving financial services industry as the country seeks to establish itself as a hub for regional finance. The panorama of the Corniche shows the recently renovated head offices of Qatar National Bank with just behind and along from it, the Ministry of Finance. The next major building is the Central Bank of Qatar, with just beyond it, and also opposite middle, the HSBC building.

in 2005 when the DSM was opened to non-nationals. Activity on the stock market slowed in 1999 as the market underwent a correction, normal after a steep rise in activity. The DSM index ended 1999 at 134.1, barely unchanged on the previous year. By early 2000, market capitalisation of the 21 companies listed on the DSM stood at just over QR18.5 billion (approximately $5.1 billion). Development of the DSM has included relocation to purpose built premises, the introduction of an electronic trading system and the opening of the market to non-GCC investors in 2005, all of which allow the DSM to play its full role in the economic life of the Emirate.

### International Events

Qatar provides all the services as a venue for the staging of international events. The Emirate enjoys excellent links to all corners of the world, international class hotels and top class exhibition, conference and sporting facilities. These facilities include hotels such as the Sheraton (the first international class hotel in Doha, opened in 1982) and Marriott. Qatar also boasts a premier exhibition and conference centre in the Qatar International Exhibition Centre (QIEC) in the West Bay area of Doha, covering 10,000 square metres. The QIEC regularly hosts business and trade exhibitions that attract executives from around the globe.

The country has become the preferred location for holding international and regional political, business and sporting events. These events provide important opportunities for Qatar to demonstrate the dynamism of its economy, the stability of its political and social environments and the excellence of its business infrastructure.

Qatar has hosted major political and business events such as the 1997 Middle East and North Africa conference – a gathering of regional and international political and business leaders that played an important role in supporting the Arab-Israeli peace process. The decision to hold the conference in Doha was a reflection of the good relations that Qatar enjoys with all states in the region. Other important regional summits held in Doha include the Organisation of Islamic Conference (OIC) foreign ministers meeting in March 1998 and OIC and GCC heads of state summits in 1997. The World Trade Organisation held its 4th Ministerial Conference in Doha in November 2001, which has become known as "The Doha Round" that generated a reaffirmation of the values and intentions of the WTO known as the "Doha Declaration". In June 2005 Qatar Played host to the Group of 77 "South-South Summit".

Qatar is also becoming an important venue for international sporting events. The Qatar Tennis Open, sponsored by the major oil company ExxonMobil has become a fixture in the international tennis tour run by the Association of Tennis Professionals – the governing body for men's tennis. The Qatar Open, hosted annually in January by the Qatar Tennis and Squash Federation, started in 1993 and attracts the world's top male

Major sporting figures such as tennis stars Tim Henman (*above*) and Mary Pierce *(below)* are attracted by the quality of the facilities offered at Doha's international tournaments.

tennis players. In 2005, the tournament offered total prize money of $975,000 for singles and doubles events.

Qatar has also become a regular fixture on the international golf tour. The Doha Golf Club offers world class facilities. In December 1998, the Qatar Masters tournament was launched as part of Professional Golfers Association (PGA) tour. Each year since has seen an expansion in depth of the field and importance to the players on tour. In 2005 the event was co-sanctioned with the Asian PGA creating a new level of competition.

Qatar's five-star hotels offer first class facilities, all under the supervisory eye of Qatar National Hotels (QNH). Seen here, anticlockwise from above and opposite are the Four Seasons, the Ritz Carlton, the Rydges, the Ramada and the Marriott.

# 8 Today's Society

## Education

In the development of the Qatari nation – where society and the State interact – the area seen as of overriding importance by the Emir, Sheikh Hamad, and his Consort, Sheikha Moza, is education. In modern Qatar, boys and girls, young men and young women, have equal access to the State education system which offers schooling from kindergarten to postgraduate level. The system as a whole and the school curricula at different levels are under constant review to ensure that they incorporate the most up-to-date knowledge and teaching methods and lead to the qualification of young nationals in the subjects required for the country's further development.

The introduction of a five-year 'Quality Qatarisation Plan' for the energy sector, in June 2000, aimed at 50 per cent Qatarisation. Parallel to that was a government programme to establish future industrial needs and to ensure that the relevant education, training and development was available for Qatari nationals. The potential of Qatar's women was not being ignored, and curricula and teaching techniques were being reviewed as extensively in the girls' schools as in the boys'. New emphasis was being placed on the teaching of science, information technology and technical subjects. English was being taught as a second language at an earlier stage than previously.

With increasing Qatarisation, the country recognised its need of qualified nationals at all levels. This has led to a re-evaluation of the technical training offered at certificate and diploma level. The education system was also encouraging students to consider such previously less favoured options either as a gateway to direct employment or to higher education.

However sophisticated it may seem today, education in Qatar began in a simple and traditional way, evolving from the local Qur'an schools. While the focus was on religious studies, the children were also taught to read and write, and were familiarised with elementary mathematics. Even in those early

The spirit of education carries a certain fervency in modern-day Qatar, where schooling of high quality is available to every young person from kindergarten to further education. At the infant level (*pictured here*) independent schools play almost as great a part as the State-sponsored structure.

days, classes were available for boys as well as girls. The first primary schools were introduced only in 1952. Since then, the development of the education system was to be rapid. One of the first ministries to be established was the Ministry of Education and Knowledge, in 1956. The basis of the modern education system was introduced in the same year, with three stages from the age of six: Primary (6 years), Preparatory (3 years) and Secondary (also 3 years). The first batch of regular students were deemed to have completed their Primary Education in 1956.

Today the Supreme Education council, under the guidance of HH Sheikha Moza, has taken on the leading role in education from the Ministry of Education, and, following a specially

commissioned study of the Qatari education system in 2001, is committed to an extensive reform of the system. The focus of this new initiative is the creation of independent schools that will work to the highest educational standards and ultimately be autonomous. Twelve such schools were founded in 2004, a further 25 came on board in 2005, and the programme is set to escalate from this energetic start. Already over-subscribed, the new fee-paying schools have proved to be immensely popular with parents and students alike.

Schools are closely monitored and regularly evaluated using a rigorous set of standards that focus on modern teaching methods (in place of the traditional rote learning previously widely practiced). This is controlled by the Evaluation

Institutute who see their role as not simply informing schools, teachers and students about their performance, but also informing parents and decision makers on the extent to which schools are fulfilling their roles. This encourages parents to make informed decisions on their choice of schools, and effectively introduces a 'free market' approach where schools compete for excellence.

Teacher training, essential in achieving and maintaining the anticipated standards, has been a cornerstone of the development, working closely with the Evaluation Institute who monitor standards.

Most expatriate communities have private schools offering their own national curriculum – either in entirety or in modified form. Each

With the presence of sophisticated expatriate communities in temporary residence in Qatar, a cosmopolitan element has entered much of senior education – as exemplified by the three students (*left*) of Doha English Speaking School, attired in the national dress of their various Qatari, Scottish and South Asian communities.

At play school age, boys and girls mix together. The overall aim is to have introduced elementary literacy before advancing to the primary stage.

foreign embassy is permitted to sponsor one non-profit making community school, which can build its own facilities on land allocated for the purpose by the Emir and the government.

Specialised schools include the Religious Institute, Technical and Scientific Secondary Schools and the Secondary School of Commerce, as well as establishments catering to children with special needs. Facilities are open to both nationals and expatriates. In addition to developing the capabilities of children with, for example, Down's Syndrome or Cerebral Palsy, there are schools in the State sector for those with sight or hearing problems. A new, state-of-the-art facility, Shafallah Centre, opened in 1999 under the auspices of the Supreme Council for Family Affairs, and its National Committee for Special Needs. It would in due course provide therapy, stimulation and education to handicapped children from birth to the age of 18, and provide support to their families. It would also specialise in the education of autistic children. The Centre has a spectacular state-of-the-art sensory stimulation centre. The Supreme Council, headed by Sheikha Moza, Consort of the Emir, reports directly to the Council of Ministers.

## Qatar University

Qatar University, founded in 1973, developed out of the State's two teacher training colleges, one for men and another for women. It later moved to a purpose-built campus on the northern fringes of Doha and currently has seven faculties: Education; Humanities and Social Studies; Science; Shari'a and Islamic Studies; Engineering; Administration and Economics; and Technology. There are also four

research centres at the university; Scientific and Applied Research; Humanities and Documentation; Educational Research; and Biography and Sunna Research Centre. The university also has a Computer Centre, Educational Technology Centre, Gulf Co-operation Council Development Studies project and a technical Development Bureau. The Marine Biology department has its own research vessel and works in co-operation with the Aquarium Section at Qatar National Museum to document and monitor marine life in the Gulf.

Both Qatari nationals and expatriate Arabic speakers have access to the university where some 8,500 students were enrolled in the year 2000. There are parallel facilities for men and women, with separate campuses. Almost all courses are equally available to both sexes although some additional facilities are still to be developed to open up such subjects as engineering to the female students. Female students outnumber their male counterparts by almost three to one.

While the educational standard of the country's women is high, it must also be remembered that a greater proportion of male students go abroad for higher education overseas.

As with other sectors, the university was undertaking a Qatarisation programme in the later 1990s. In 2000, 44 per cent of the 791 teaching staff were Qatari nationals, as were 78 per cent of the 882 administrative staff.

Qatari graduates are often sent abroad on scholarships to study for their Master's degrees or for a Doctorate, attending universities in Britain, USA, Japan and France. The university has also introduced a parallel education system enabling government employees to complete their studies in the evenings. In keeping with the country's requirements in the industrial and business sectors, new specialisations have been introduced in information sciences, communications, data systems, and gas engineering.

Qatar has been a pioneer in Geographic Information Systems (GIS), becoming the first country in the world to introduce it on a national scale; as a result, it acts as a regional GIS training centre. The university has also introduced courses in agricultural sciences. It was to issue early in the new millennium an 11-volume Arab Environmental Encyclopaedia, in a project funded by the Emir – one of the most important international publications on sustainable development.

State education receives increasing support from the private sector. Banks, commercial establishments and the energy sector finance the construction of new lecture and seminar halls, laboratories, language laboratories, computer suites and other facilities both at school and university level.

Literacy rates are high in the country. Catering for the needs of those who dropped out of school or otherwise missed out on earlier education, the State undertakes direct supervision of literacy and adult education programmes, in which over 3,000 students were enrolled in 1999.

A Language Institute, established in 1973, continues to offer courses in Arabic, English and French for government, official and semi-official organisations in the county. A Department of Vocational Development and Training, founded back in 1962, has also encouraged young Qatari women to train in office and secretarial studies. Many of the girls have gone on to work in the tele-communications and energy sectors.

The government takes every opportunity to stress the importance of education in preparing its nationals for the challenges of the new millennium. In that vein, it is also prepared to constantly review the standards and scope of facilities in the country, seeking outside technical advice from specialised United Nations bodies or from other countries with specialised expertise wherever it is considered appropriate.

## Qatar Foundation

Qatar Foundation for Education, Science and Community Development is a private, chartered, nonprofit organization, founded in 1995 by His Highness Sheikh Hamad Bin Khalifa Al-Thani. Guided by the principle that a nation's greatest resource is the potential of its people, the aim of Qatar Foundation has

Qatar University's rooftops *(opposite)* are a variation on the theme of the traditional Gulf wind towers – although all indoor premises enjoy modern airconditioning. The importance of ensuring a well educated younger generation *(below and opposite)* is increasingly the focus of government initiatives.

Qatar University, founded in 1973, has seven faculties and four research centres. For all students, the computer (*below*) is the essential transmissional tool.

been to develop that potential through a network of centres devoted to progressive education, research and community welfare.

Supported by abundant residential and recreational facilities, Education City is envisioned as a community of institutions that serve the whole citizen, from early childhood education to post-graduate study.

Most students are citizens or residents of Qatar, but many come from other countries in the Gulf and throughout the Middle East with some from beyond the Arab World.

Another part of the Foundation is Qatar Science and Technology Park, a massive, state-of-the-art convention centre with a shopping centre to serve the growing number of students, staff and faculty living on site.

A central library, a student centre, a club for staff and faculty, a ceremonial entrance, and a golf course all form part of the ongoing development of the Foundation, as well as a 350-bed, all-digital Specialty Teaching Hospital – a world-class facility offering general care and specializing in women's and children's health.

New educational programmes are constantly being sought, including a school of communications and journalism, and an Islamic studies centre. All of these will be provided with purpose-built facilities.

A range of further local programmes abound. The Learning Centre caters for children who are failing to reach their full potential, with the aim that they should ultimately return to mainstream education. It also offers courses for gifted children. The Foundation's Family Development Centre provides training to women of low-income groups, helping them acquire or hone skills within the context of Qatar's social and cultural norms, such as will enable them (for example) to set up or participate in small businesses securing economic independence which will help them meet the needs of their families – tailoring and embroidery, catering, office services and the like.

Qatar Academy, another part of the Foundation, comprises a co-educational Junior Academy and a segregated Senior Academy (but with a co-educational sixth form). It offers a modified British National Curriculum, to include subjects such as the history of Qatar, the Gulf, Middle East and Islamic world, and also Islamic Studies. The Academy has highly qualified staff and the finest facilities and equipment. It was looking towards accreditation with the European Council of International Schools.

Qatar University was established in 1973 and was one of the first in the region. The University has a student body of 8,500 – of which the majority are currently female.

Another component of the Foundation is the Shaqab Institute for Girls. SIG, as it is widely known, is the first educational establishment in the region to offer courses for young Qatari, Gulf and Middle Eastern women in a fuller appreciation of their culture traditions and heritage, in the context of modern technology. Music and art, interior decor and home management play their part for both day and residential students, to meet the demands and responsibilities they may face as women, wives and mothers in, for example, diplomatic or corporate life.

Close by, around a connected campus that is developing into something of a global educational village, is Shaqab College of Design Arts, a daughter institute of the USA's Virginia Commonwealth University School of Arts. It prepares students for the Bachelor of Fine Arts Degree in Communication, Arts and Design (Graphic Design), Fashion Design and Merchandising, and Interior Design.

A separate entity within the Foundation, and one which straddles the boundaries between health and education, is the Qatar Diabetes Association. It aims to educate existing diabetic patients and their families about the nature of the disease and its management as well as heightening community awareness of the problem, identifying those at risk, and fostering research.

Students at the Qatar Foundation *(below)* study in branch universities whose standards are maintained by independent international educational institutions with a name to uphold. The design is substantially the work of Isukai, the renowned Japanese architect, with innovative polyhedron lecture halls *(right)* and modern student accommodation *(below right)*.

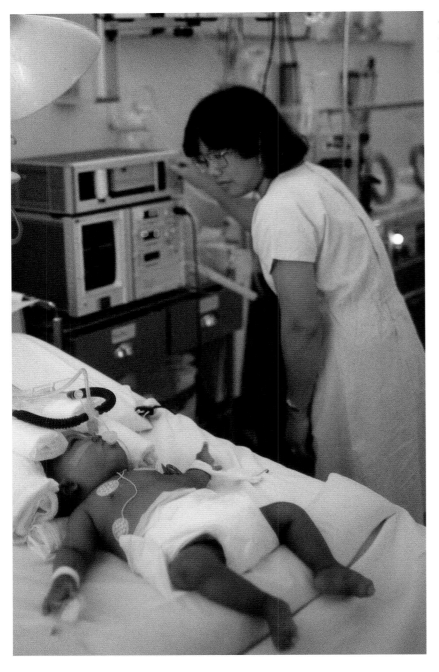

A patient is treated and monitored by a nurse trained in the use of advanced equipment at Rumaillah Hospital.

The departments of Doha's Women's Hospital (*left*) include obstetrics, gynaecology, and neo-natal intensive care. It has a world-class assisted conception unit (ACU).

## Health

The health sector has come a long way to provide the most advanced medical equipment and qualified cadres as well as expand the cover of health services all over the country through a wide network of hospitals and health centres. Health services in Qatar are discharged through a compact link chain from primary to intensive care and from health centres and major hospitals.

The National Health Authority (NHA) was established in 2005 in order to assume the highest authority in the domain of health care and replace the Ministry of Health which has been abolished by an Emiri Decree. It shall have a corporate status and a budget affiliated to the State's general budget. The NHA is affiliated to the Council of Ministers.

It aims at providing the highest quality health care possible, medical preventive and treatment services and supervising the provision of public health services at home and the medical treatment of Qatari nationals abroad. Besides, it regulates the marketing and manufacturing of drugs in accordance with international quality standards, within the framework of the public policy of the State and in accordance with a national strategy aimed at realizing the above-mentioned objectives.

The National Health Authority also supervises Hamad Medical Corporation, Hamad Specialist and Educational Hospital, private medical facilities, laboratories, pharmacies, councils of auxiliary medical professions, hospitals, primary health care centres and other public medical treatment utilities. The National Health Authority undertakes the organization of the medical private sector and it acts in coordination with the Health Insurance System to upgrade the level of health service and disseminate health education and awareness.

The development achieved in the health and medical field, besides the country's high standard of living, has led to the total eradication of several diseases such as polio, lockjaw, diphtheria, tetanus, whooping cough and meningitis from Qatar. The death rate of children was reduced significantly. A report from the general secretariat of the GCC ministers of health indicated that Qatar has less mothers' deaths ratio than any other GCC country.

Qataris holding senior medical and administrative posts in the field of health services make up 73% of the total workforce of this field in Qatar. The NHA encourages the establishment of private medical service facilities; so much so, now they represent 68% of all the

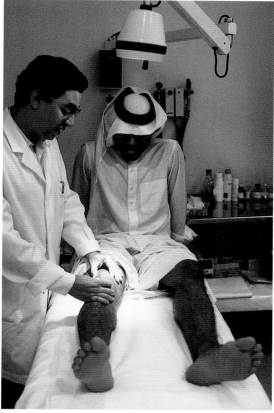

country's health services providers. The council of ministers has issued a decision to allow the investment of GCC capital in health services in the state of Qatar.

The medical cadres in the state of Qatar, 65% of whom are MDs and 56% dentists, represent 68% of the total human resources working in the medical field. Nurses are 2,919, making up 11% of the total medical workforce.

### Preventive Health Care Services

The Preventive Health Department is responsible for fighting contagious diseases; carrying out vaccination, immunization and food and quarantine watch control; providing health education in the field of mother and child care and insuring environmental health and safety. A section for incommunicable diseases was set up comprising three units: tobacco control unit, chronic diseases and accidents control and statistics unit, and nutrition unit.

### Primary Health Care

The Primary Health Services Department of Hamad Medical Corporation (HMC) supervises 23 primary health care centres, which are conveniently distributed across the country. It provides various programs including health awareness; child and mother care; immunization against child diseases; diagnostic and treatment

services of common and chronic diseases; medicines; nutritious food; clean water and ambulance and emergency services.

### Hamad Medical City

The Athletes' village has been specifically designed to be used after the Asian Games Doha 2006 to introduce a first class Medical City. This multi-million dollar building complex is built on a 34- hectare site situated adjacent to the Hamad Medical Hospital – a primary location in the centre of Doha, giving easy access to the venues and information centres for the residents of the Village. The site is to host the NHA, training facilities and four new hospitals with 1,100 beds. There will be housing for doctors and for nurses, with 871 apartments planned inside the Medical City. There will be separate recreational clubs for the doctors and nurses with the first rate swimming pools, gyms, tennis courts and other amenities.

### Health Commission Services

The Health Commission Department carries out medical checks on everybody entering the country for work or visit, and issues certificates of health fitness for such categories as those who are about to get married and who are applying for jobs, universities or public housing.

With an exceptionally high birthrate among Qatari nationals, the maternity and obstetrics sections of Qatar's hospitals play an outstanding role. *Above left,* a proud father carefully transports his recently arrived offspring, in Dukhan's Medical Centre.

## Sport and Leisure

Qatar's sophisticated sports infrastructure caters for both water and land sports. The facilities are available to nationals and expatriates alike and in many cases also to visitors. The name of Qatar has now become familiar around the world as host to international world-class sporting events, and the country has developed an enviable reputation amongst sportsmen and women for its hospitality and organisational competence.

Qatari sportsmen, meanwhile, compete in increasing numbers in local, regional and international competitions. Qatar's passion for soccer is reflected in the sixteen clubs dotted around the capital and in other towns, each boasting a grass-pitched, well-lit stadium. The six most modern clubs are each capable of seating 15,000 spectators and have an athletics track, indoor sports hall, gymnasium, tennis and squash courts, practice pitches, club rooms and, in some cases, swimming pools. The football clubs are affiliated to the Youth Authority, (YA) formed in 1990, which also sponsors clubs, societies and associations promoting motor and marine sports, athletics, tennis, table tennis, squash, bowling, Thai boxing, boxing, golf, swimming, volleyball, handball, basketball, martial arts, wrestling, weight lifting, shooting, cricket, billiards and snooker, chess, and stamp collecting.

Responsible for youth welfare in the country, the Authority YA is the counterpart of other similar bodies such as the ministries of youth, supreme councils for youth and sports etc. in other countries; and it aims to draw up the general policy for youth welfare and prepare the leaders required to implement the programs that could bring about integration and equilibrium in the society and create good citizenry.

The responsibilities of the Authority include establishing and organizing clubs, associations and youths and sports establishments and facilities. As well as endorsing encouragement awards and incentives for scientific activities. They also approve the financial estimates required for the establishment and support of projects, activities and studies related to the youths and recommend youths and sports

No country - except, perhaps, in the South Pacific - engages in any contest like Qatar's annual collective race of long boats, pictured *above* and *below*.

legislation. The Authority carries out its duties in collaboration with concerned government agencies and semi-government sports establishments such as Qatar National Olympic Committee and sports federations.

The Youth Hostel, in the Al Laqta area of Doha, offers facilities to young men travelling through the region. Qatar has, for many years, hosted a number of regional and international sporting events. October 2000 will have marked the first time it has hosted a Formula 1 World Championship Powerboat Race staged in Doha Bay.

Khalif International Tennis and Squash Complex, built in 1992, has been seen by millions around the world during the television coverage of the Qatar Open Tennis Championship. The Centre Court seats 4,500 spectators, whilst the two outer courts can each accommodate 750. There are also several practice Courts. Al Dana Club, on the same complex, has a gym, fitness centre and swimming pool and the newly developed banqueting hall hosts product launches and corporate events as well as wedding receptions and other large-scale gatherings. An indoor pool and indoor tennis courts were to have been added to the facilities before the end of the year 2000.

Camel riding *(above)*, once a necessity of desert life, is now a leisure activity for many of the country's youth.

Performance cars of varying kinds are popular in Qatar, either in the desert outskirts *(below right)*, or for dune bashing in the sands of Khor Al Udaid *(below)*. The Corniche, with its sweeping curve and wide borders for spectators, has proved ideal for motor and cycle races *(left and right)*, events first staged in 2003.

The Equestrian Club and events such as the annual International Show Jumping Championships (*left*) sustain the peninsula's long love affair with the horse, particularly the Arabian horse (*below*).

Doha Golf Club, with the country's first grass course, opened in 1996 and hosts the annual Qatar Masters, a PGA European Tour event. The club has both an 18-hole championship course and a nine-hole floodlit Academy course. Designed by Peter Harradine, the classic links course has taken advantage of the natural variations in terrain and outcrops of limestone, and an ambitious landscaping programme has turned a previously barren area of desert into a veritable oasis with date palms, huge cacti and colourful plants. The eight artificial lakes provide irrigation for the course, but also act as water hazards. The first nine holes, whilst slightly shorter than the second nine, are unique in design and require real accuracy. Both professionals and beginners enjoy playing at the Doha Golf Club. The environment is one which the non-golfer can enjoy too. The elegant clubhouse has a good Pro Shop; the restaurants, which are also open to non-members, have achieved a high reputation. The club was aiming over time to develop into a fully-fledged Country Club with additional non-golfing facilities. Work on a leisure centre including a swimming pool, Jacuzzi, sauna, fitness centre and children's indoor play area was completed in January 2001. To sit out on the verandahs overlooking the course is to bask in greenness and tranquillity. Meanwhile the course attracts a variety of wildlife, all of which has been documented. Two other well-established golf courses, both oil-on-sand, continue to attract players, one in Messaieed the other in Dukhan.

Khalifa Sports City, known previously as Khalifa Stadium has hosted international athletics meetings, regional, international and world events. The football stadium - which hosted the World Youth Championship, has a 40,000 seat capacity, whilst the indoor sports hall can seat 1,800. There are, in addition, practice pitches and an extensive sports medicine centre. A recent addition to the complex is an Olympic size swimming pool,prominent in events at the Asian Games in 2006.

Traditional sports have not been forgotten. Equestrian events figure prominently in the sporting calendar, with local and international equestrian Desert Marathons held in the Messaieed beachfront area. Jumping, racing and show events - local, regional and international - are held at the Al Rayyan race track and showground of the Race and Equestrian Club, which also trains young riders. The Camel Race Committee administers the local and regional programmes at Al Shahaniyah Race Track. The YA oversees both the Race and Equestrian Club and the Camel Race Committee. Al Shaqab Stud of H.H. the Emir also has a private riding club, offering tuition in basic skills, showjumping and dressage to both children and adults.

Many of the hotels and recreation clubs offer sports coaching, and run various league and club events. There is a wide choice of private gyms, fitness and health clubs which cater specifically to men or women, or offer separate timings for the two groups. Sailing clubs in Doha, Al Khor and Dukhan offer tuition as well as organising regular races. Cricket is gaining in popularity, and a number of other sports are often played informally by groups setting up temporary pitches on open land.

Expatriate schools participate in a number of inter-school competitions, and State schools – for both boys and girls – run sports, health and fitness programmes. Qatar University has its own extensive sporting facilities, available separately to both male and female students.

## The Arts

In addition to those facilities offered through the Youth Authority, there are numerous facilities for arts, photography and drama in the country. A new National Council for Arts, Heritage and Culture administers the Qatar National Theatre. The theatre itself is available to local and international groups for theatrical and musical performances. There are several Qatari theatre troupes and a thriving expatriate amateur theatre, the Doha Players' Theatre. Two art galleries in Al Bida Park frequently host exhibitions of art, craft and photography by local and expatriate artists. The Qatar Fine Arts Society encourages young artists of all nationalities, and runs a series of workshops. It also provides workshop facilities for local craftsmen.

The Department of Art Education at the University holds frequent exhibitions of oil and watercolour paintings, silk painting, ceramics, woodwork, metalwork and weaving by female students. Government encourages the revival of traditional craft skills as well as the acquisition and development of new objéts d'art. A special youth centre for creative arts has opened, attracting a large number of young people of all nationalities.

Several literary competitions attract national and expatriate writers, both of short stories and poetry and talented local playwrights have emerged.

Doha's golf course (*right and above*) is of international excellence, attracting world players.

Surrounded on all sides by the warm shallow waters of the Gulf, the Qataris have in recent years taken increasingly to water sports – powerboat racing in Doha bay, a sailing race as a prelude to the hosting of the Asian Games 2006, a proud waterskier bearing the national flag.

Qatar's National Day - September 3rd - is a public holiday, climaxed by a pagent in the National Stadium (*shown overleaf*), for which the participants train and rehearse throughout the preceding twelve months.

### Doha Asian Games

The hosting of the 15th Asian Games in Doha in December 2006, the second largest international sporting event after the International Summer Olympic Games, has provided wider opportunities which Qatar's authorities have not been slow to maximise. In the words of Mr Abdulla Al-Qahtani,

Director General of the Doha Asian Games Organising Committee, 'Everything built for the Games revolves around the framework of our national development plans; that is to construct new permanent venues only after we carefully study and approve their post-games use with related organisations.'

The Games have come a long way since the inaugural games in New Delhi in1951 welcomed 11 countries playing in just six sports. Now 55 years later, the Games welcomes 45 different countries, participating in 39 competitive sports totalling 412 events – the highest ever number of events hosted at an Asian Games.

Qatar, itself the highest medal winner of the GCC, with 17 medals to its name from the 14th Asian Games, was set to perform well. The authorities have been keen to stress that the games are not just a sporting event, nor are they solely about greeting visitors to the country; they are about international brotherliness and Qatari position in the region and the world, and about the culture of which the community in Qatar is very proud.

Princess Alia of Jordan sits besides Qatar's gold medal team, winners of the 120 km horse endurance race of the Pan Arab Games of 1999.

*Left:* Qatar's 100m gold medalist Hassan Kasefi stands beside the silver medalist.

*Above, above left and below left:* The Khalifa Stadium is an impressive feat of engineering, building on the former 20,000 seat stadium to increase capacity and provide a covered area.

Doha's stadium's Olympic swimming pool provides the training facilities for Qatar's swimmers.

Qatar contests Kuwait at football in the 1998 Asian Games

December 1998, at the Asian Games, saw Qatar's Mohamed Tayyib winning the 1500m track race.

Qatar's gold medalist Salam Jaber lifted 105 kg to win the World Championship at Athens.

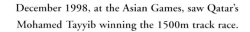

# 9 Moulding the Future

## Stephen Day CMG

The people of Qatar have good reason to face the future with confidence. Predictions are risky, especially where the fate of nations is concerned and, as Francis Bacon warned, are best kept for winter talk around the fireside rather than recorded in a book of reference. Nevertheless, the reasons for optimism are solid.

Perhaps the safest bet would be on income per head of population rising to become once again the highest in the world - and likely to stay that way for a very long time. The switch from an oil to a gas economy does not happen overnight. The North Dome Field, discovered in the seventies, has required decades of study and negotiation, huge investments and state-of-the-art engineering to bring into production. Shipments of Liquefied Natural Gas now flow regularly to the Far East, paying off the enormous capital costs and soon bringing the national budget into a healthy surplus.

A gas-based economy will eventually insulate the budget against the dramatic swings characteristic of the oil market. In 1998, for example, Qatar's Gross Domestic Product fell by 7.4 per cent: then rose 8.9 per cent the following year. Gas revenues based on long-term supply contracts will increasingly dominate the State's revenues and provide a firm basis for the future economy. A new generation of technology is now being developed on an industrial scale by Shell and others to produce liquids direct from gas (GTL). The further one looks into the future the more solid gas revenues look. Innovations in car technology and world-wide demands to clean up our environment make gas the fuel of the future. In America, as one example, gas supplies no longer outpace demand and prices have shot up. Hitherto, LNG made up a mere 1 per cent of America's gas; that proportion is now likely to quadruple. In the Far East, traditionally the main consumer of LNG, demand will continue to rise, with the prospect of the world's most populous country, China, coming into the market as the pollution from its old coal-fired power-stations becomes intolerable.

The prospect of great wealth brings dangers as well as rewards, and Qatar has for some time been preparing for the new era.

Nevertheless, priority has gone to internal stability and preservation of Qatar's unique social patterns. To an outsider it is easy to regard

At the fourth Middle East and North Africa (MENA) Conference, which Qatar hosted, delegates of 61 nations attended.

the smaller Gulf states as similar. Dress is uniform, hydrocarbons are the main source of wealth, Islam is the universal religion, the people are conservative. Yet behind these general characteristics lie great variations in attitudes and behaviour, and Qatar has always retained a unique personality, more modest, relaxed, with a strong sense of community, determined to defend its values against the pressures of westernisation and consumerism.

This strength of character, the determination not to be submerged by tides of foreign influence, has been a consistent pattern throughout Qatar's contacts with the outside world. Persians, Ottomans, other Arabs, British have each in turn been accommodated as visitors, given a good meal and encouraged firmly but politely to push off and leave Qatar to run its own affairs. It was not until the late 1940s that foreign residents began to stay in Qatar at the beginning of the oil boom, and these mainly on the west coast, well away from the main towns.

Never part of anyone's empire, Qatar did its own thing.

Qatari society evolved and indeed was

strengthened by extraordinary swings in political and economic circumstances over the past century. A traditional economy based on pearling, trade and herding was shattered first by the development of the cultured pearl, followed shortly after by the Second World War. Famine was averted by emergency supplies shipped in by friendly allies.

It would be impossible for today's young, whether Arab or foreign, to conceive the harshness of that life, summed up during an encounter in the air-conditioned office of Doha's leading jeweller with an old pearler. The writer, then British Ambassador, referred naively to the good old days. Fixing the diplomat with a look of withering disdain the wiry old man responded – 'For you, young man, half an hour then would be like a life-time of hell.'

Then came oil, the foundation of a modern state, development of a well laid-out capital city around the curving bay of Doha, an excellent education system that attracted students from less developed neighbouring Gulf countries, foreign travel, large-scale immigration and – less welcome – two major Gulf wars, revolution in neighbouring Iran and huge swings in oil

The opening ceremony of the fourth MENA Conference, meeting in Doha, is addressed by HH Sheikh Hamad Bin
Khalifa Al Thani, Emir of Qatar, whose image is simultaneously projected on a massive screen at the conference centre.

revenues. That these unpredictable, often dramatic changes strengthened the cohesiveness of this small, rich society is due above all to the staunch Islamic faith of the Qatari people and their commitment to family. The senior official or top businessman will find time for his devotional and family obligations, and the Westerner should understand that, faced with the competing demands of a social event and a customary daily visit to mother and father, most Qataris will give the reception a miss and put parents first.

Sheikh Hamad Bin Khalifa has built on the foundations laid down by his father, preparing Qatar for a new era and new challenges. His leadership is unquestioned. The policies and practices of new Qatar have emerged from far-reaching debates that he has led, and the changes are extensive.

In foreign affairs, Qatar remains fully committed to its regional and international alliances but has shown itself prepared to take an independent stand, as over the Yemeni civil war of 1994/5 when Qatar's support, against the GCC majority, for those fighting to preserve Yemeni unity was proved justified after the first gulf war.

These changes have been introduced within a wider package of reforms, the most striking of which has been the satellite television channel 'Al-Jazeera', now broadcasting the most widely watched programmes among Arabs in Europe and from Morocco to Yemen. Sheikh Hamad's government has opened a door that brings a gust of fresh air into Arab political debate. One of his first acts as ruler was to close down the Ministry of Information, with the

HH the Emir, Sheikh Hamad Bin Khalifa Al Thani, was invited by President Bush of the United States to Washington to discuss Middle Eastern and world energy affairs.

observation that the main function of such Ministries in the Arab world was not to inform but to censor, and Qatar had no need for such nannying.

Highly professional in its product, Al-Jazeera's talk shows tackle hitherto taboo subjects such as human rights, torture, banned political groups and rival interpretations of Islamic teaching. Other Arab governments have been quick to complain, even to withdraw Ambassadors, but as a *Newsweek* review, quoting an American author of a study on satellite television's impact on the Middle East, concluded: 'This is the beginning of a fundamental change.' 'Free expression is a human right,' said the Chairman of Al-Jazeera, Sheikh Hamad bin Thamer Al Thani. 'It is difficult to control information when the world has become a small village.' Broadcasting the truth on sensitive, topical issues has attracted an enthusiastic audience among Arabs numbed by decades of officially approved news churned out by national television stations.

In parallel with the encouragement of debate have come advances in women's rights and wider public participation in government. In March 1999 the first elections were held for 29 municipal districts. The move is intended as a first step towards a fully elected Assembly. Women were encouraged both to vote and to stand for office. A panel of wives of Qatari notables briefed meetings of women on their rights and obligations, urging them to measure up to their new responsibilities. Behind this step lay recognition of the way in which Qatari women had seized the opportunities offered by public education, to a point where by the year 2000 women had come to outnumber men at the state

university and to win the lion's share of academic prizes. Women control substantial financial resources; the first women's bank in the Gulf was established in Doha, and women are increasingly found working in public departments and commercial concerns.

These reforms in the role and responsibilities of women should not be seen as westernisation. A conference convened in Doha shortly after the new Emir took over encouraged a public debate on how women could reaffirm those extensive rights that are enshrined in Islamic doctrine, while avoiding threats to family life and the many problems encountered in other advanced societies. Speakers were invited from around the world, and men were encouraged to join in and test pre-conceived notions.

Women's assertion of their right to play a full part in decision-making and the work-place recalls to a certain extent their role in traditional Arabian society. As many commentators have pointed out, where subservience among women is encountered in certain Moslem countries, this is evidence not of Islam but of mere 'male chauvinism'. Islam provided a legal and moral basis for an extensive body of women's rights long before such thoughts became current in the West. In addition, Qatari women can point proudly to their bedouin traditions, as when they fought side by side with their menfolk in the battle of Wajba that resulted in the expulsion of Ottoman forces from the peninsula.

To call all these reforms 'democracy' could be misleading. Rooted in well-established Islamic tradition, sheikhly rule is proving both flexible and relevant to modern trends. Change is being led from the top, the pace determined after careful consultation with all sections of

At a meeting with the ruler of Qatar's most immediate maritime neighbour, Bahrain, Sheikh Hamad Bin Isa Al Khalifa (on the right) HH Sheikh Hamad of Qatar discussed issues which unite and divide the two countries.

Qatar's Foreign Minister, Hamad Bin Jassem (Bin Jabor Al Thani, the First Deputy Prime Minister and Minister of Foreign Affairs (*left*) addresses the 2nd South Summit of the Grouof 77 held in Doha in June 2005.

towards greater participation in political decisions and more openness in government.

No ruler today has a sinecure; the demands and cares of office are constant and unpredictable. Sheikh Hamad has led the way in encouraging more openness, while insisting that obligations as well as privileges must be shared. He has urged his people not to look to the state for every bounty but to join in the creation of wealth. The permanent consitution has already been endorsed and is now in force. The country is looking forward to forming an elected assembly.

Most responsible Qataris would agree that the greatest challenge lies in reforming the educational system. Not only is Qatar a young country, its population is heavily tilted towards youth, half being aged sixteen or under. Supported by his remarkable consort, Sheikha Moza Al Misnad, Sheikh Hamad has set out to lift the overall educational standards of the new generation in a step change. Traditional education in the Arab world was essentially authoritative – sit there, learn this, repeat after me. If Qatar is to flourish and especially if it is to use its gas wealth for the benefit of future generations, the young must be encouraged to innovate, to think for themselves, and above all to develop enterprise – to diversify the economy and create new commercial ventures.

The young Heir Apparent, Sheikh Tamim Bin Hamad, has no doubt that improvements in the educational system should be top of the Government's responsibilities. Being himself fully representative of his contemporaries and knowing their concerns and aspirations, he is well qualified to speak for the younger generation. He also has a deep commitment to preserving the environment, especially the need to preserve the beaches and open spaces

of Qatar so that families can enjoy the simple leisure pursuits that are part of their traditional way of life.

Spearheading the educational revolution is the Qatar Foundation for Education, Science and Community Development chaired by the Amir's Consort, Sheikha Moza, mother of the Heir Apparent. Launched as one of the first initiatives of the new ruler, the aim of the Foundation is to mould future citizens who combine deeply rooted attachment to their Islamic and Arab identity with pride in their past and an ability to draw on those aspects of technological and scientific progress that will benefit both their country and the wider world. It is a hugely ambitious endeavour and the results to date have been impressive.

On the historic site outside Doha, where Qataris defeated the Ottoman forces, an ambitious new campus has been laid out for what will become an Education City. Already the Qatar Academy houses kindergarten through to Advanced stream, teaching in Arabic and English to British GCSE and 'A' level standards. Entry is strictly by merit, with blind entry tests supervised by specialists from abroad. Classes are mixed, boys and girls, through kindergarten and junior and again at the senior level. The campus also houses a Learning Centre for children with special needs, the Shaqab College of Design Arts (a branch of the Commonwealth of Virginia College), an indoor sports complex and the administration of the Foundation. Plans are being put in place for a new University with Medical School, Hospital and colleges of engineering, Management and Science together with a Museum, College of International Affairs and Diplomacy, and a Science Park.

Some of the brightest children in the new Academy are from the ruling family. The complexity of this very Arabian community is little understood in the West. It is not feudal and it is certainly not autocratic. No-one who has met Sheikh Hamad bin Khalifah or seen him on and off duty could regard him as a tyrant. He has devoted three decades to preparing for these responsibilities, knows and is known by his people, and has a shrewd concept of Qatar's place in the world.

This outcome was not inevitable. In the 1960s, when the writer first came to Arabia, received wisdom in the West was that the days of the traditional rulers were numbered. Hurricane winds were blowing across Africa and Asia. 'Modern' was widely seen as republican, perhaps in military uniform. Today, with the arrival of hereditary republicanism in the region, opposite conclusions are being reached. With the passing of the twentieth century, traditional regimes were showing unusual vigour. Transfers of power to young, educated, forward-looking and above all self-confident Arab rulers seem to be setting a pattern originated by Sheikh Hamad.

Some contemporary academic writing has commented on the trend. Michael Harb, Assistant Professor at Georgia State University, in his work *All in the Family – Absolutism,* *Revolution and Democracy in the Middle Eastern Monarchies,* analysed in some detail how 'these monarchies may be able to combine their traditional institutions with ones more modern – or more liberal – than those found in most other countries in the region.'

Rooted in unquestioned religious principles, and norms of social behaviour that have evolved over hundreds, perhaps thousands of years, the sheikhly dynasties have shown themselves to be more flexible, more responsive and more tolerant than the regimes thrown up by revolution or military coup. Qatar has undergone changes as significant as any experienced elsewhere in Asia, yet without sacrificing its unique identity. The transition has been organic, not revolutionary.

Living in a tough neighbourhood, with a harsh climate and rugged environment, the Qataris will need the faith and resilience of their ancestors. Their many friends will also hope that they retain their good humour and sound common sense, as well as that greatest of all Arabian traditions, warm hospitality. The ownership of abundant natural resources of energy imposes heavy obligations. Without pretending to be a world power, Qatar has become a nation of international importance. All the indications are that Qatar is well able to discharge its commitments.

Delegates of rulers and leading ministers from neighbouring countries gather in Doha *(below)* for a meeting of the Gulf Co-operation Council, to which Qatar's Foreign Minister, Hamad Bin Jassem, *(below, right)* contributed his forward thinking.

The "Doha Debates" staged at the Qatar Foundation
*(below)* and broadcast internationally, have bravely
confronted contentious issues such as the future of secular
government in the Muslim world and the equality of
women in Arab society, topics long skirted by the region's
media.

# Bibliography

**Al-Othman, Nasser** With Their Bare Hands: The Story of the Oil Industry in Qatar, Longman, 1984

**Batouny, K.H.** Ecology and Flora of Qatar, University of Qatar,1981

**Bibby, Geoffrey** Looking For Dilmun, [Reprinted] Stacey International, 1996

**Birch, A., J. Gale,** Field Guide to the Birds of the Middle East, Poyser, 1996

**Bulloch, John** The Gulf: A Portrait of Kuwait, Qatar, Bahrain and the U.A.E., Century Publishing, 1984

**Collas, E. & A. Taylor** Gulf Landscapes, Motivate Publishing, 1992

**de Cardi, Beatrice (Ed.)** Qatar Archaeological Report: Excavations 1973, O.U.P. 1978

**Dipper, F.** The Living Seas: Marine Life of the Southern Gulf, Motivate Publishing, 1989

**Edens, Christopher** Chiefdoms and Early States in the Near East, Monographs in World Archaeology No.18, Prehistory Press, 1994

**Edens, Christopher** Khor Ile-Sud, Qatar: The Archaeology of Late Bronze Age Purple Dye Production in the Arabian Gulf, Iraq No. 61, 1999

**Facey, William** The Boat Carvings at Jabal Al-Jussasiyah, Northeast Qatar, P.S.A.S. No 17, 1987

**Facey, William** The Story of the Eastern Province of Saudi Arabia, Stacey International, 1994

**Fouad, Ibrahim** Qatar and the Sea, Qatar National Printing Press, rev.ed. 1997

**Gallagher, M.** Snakes of the Arabian Gulf and Oman, pub. by the author, 1993

**Graz, Liesl** The Turbulent Gulf: People, Politics and Power, 1992

**Gross, Christian** Mammals of the Southern Gulf Motivate Publishing 1987

**Hawkins, D.F.** Primitive Rock Carvings in Qatar, P.S.A.S. No.17, 1987

**Hoyt, E.** Riding with the Dolphins: the Equinox Guide to Dolphins and Porpoises, Camden House, 1992

**Jongbloed, Marijke** The Living Desert, Motivate Publishing, 1988

**Kapel, Holger** Atlas of the Stone-Age Cultures of Qatar, Jutland Archaeological Society, 1967

**Kelly, J.B.** Britain and the Persian Gulf, Oxford, 1968

**Lorimer, J.G.** Gazetteer of the Persian Gulf, Oman and Central Arabia, Calcutta, 1908-15

**Osborne, Patrick E. (Ed.)** Desert Ecology of Abu Dhabi, Pisces Publications, 1996

**Palgrave, W.G.** Narrative of a Year's Journey through Central and Eastern Arabia, London 1877

**Potts, D.T.** The Arabian Gulf in Antiquity: Vol 1, Clarendon Press, Oxford, 1990

**Rice, Michael** The Archaeology of the Arabian Gulf, Routledge, 1994

**Robinson, D.** Birds of Southern Arabia, Motivate Publishing, 1992

**Saroufim, Nabil** Zubara and Murwab: A Report on the Recent Excavations [In Arabic], Ministry of Information, Qatar, 1987

**Tixier, Jacques (Ed.)** Mission Archeologique Francaise à Qatar, Tome 1 1980, Tome 2 1988, Ministry of Information, Qatar

**Vine, Peter** The Heritage of Qatar, Immel Publishing, 1992

**Walker, D.** Insects of Eastern Arabia, Macmillan

**Zahlan, Rosemarie Said** The Creation of Qatar, Croom Helm, London, 1978

# Index

Numbers in italics refer to pages on which relevant illustrations
fall, sometimes together with textual references.  References are
limited to major, rather than passing, mentions to avoid long
strings of numbers.